Social Studies Content

for the

Elementary School Teacher

Gloria T. Alter
Northern Illinois University

Jay Monson
Utah State University

Bruce E. Larson
Western Washington University

Jack Morgan
University of Louisville

Merrill,
an imprint of Prentice Hall
Upper Saddle River, New Jersey   Columbus, Ohio

Editor: Bradley J. Potthoff
Development Editor: Gianna Marsella
Production Editor: JoEllen Gohr
Cover Designer: Karrie Converse-Jones
Production Manager: Pamela D. Bennett
Director of Marketing: Kevin Flanagan
Marketing Manager: Meghan Shepherd
Marketing Coordinator: Krista Groshong

Printed in the United States of America

10 9 8 7 6 5 4 3 2 1

ISBN: 0-13-022480-4

Social Studies Content

for the

Elementary School Teacher

Table of Contents:

HISTORY

Dr. Gloria T. Alter
Northern Illinois University

Recent book titles reveal the crisis and controversy in historical literacy--*Don't Know Much About History?; Historical Literacy; History in the Schools: What Shall We Teach?; History on Trial; Lies My Teacher Told Me; The New American History; A Different Mirror: A History of Multicultural America;* and more. While the field of history is hardly alone in this literacy crisis, it is perhaps the hardest hit as the "most contentious field of the curriculum" (National Center for History in the Schools, 1996, p. ix). Questions are raised as to whose history matters and whose voices and experiences will be heard and why. This chapter briefly examines the dynamic and challenging subject matter of history, as it is addressed in the grades K-6 curriculum. The history standards provide a framework for exploration. But first, an introduction to history.

What Is History and Why Is It Important?

It has been said that "Life is lived forward, but it is understood backward" (Kierkegaard). Without an understanding of the past, citizens cannot make sense of the present and make wise decisions regarding political, social, and moral issues. The past is not left behind as the present is created and lived. It is carried with us to guide and direct our behavior.

History is not a romanticized view of the past. Neither is it an understanding of the past once and for all, created at some particular time in our collective past. Textbooks from as late as the sixties and seventies contain romanticized views of such topics as slavery and the Ku Klux Klan, which are at odds with what citizens now know to be true (Nash, 1998).

History is the human race's past. "Huge portions of the world" and "numerous people in our own country" are not left out in responsible attempts at writing history. As it turns out, "our roots are more complex than we sometimes think them to be and more complex than historians [have] allowed them to be" (Nash, 1998). History addresses both the tragedies and the triumphs of our lives, and to include both does not diminish either.

History plays a socializing role in our culture and as such, it is an observably important aspect of the curriculum. Guidelines about what is most important for children to know about our past and the world's past are provided in the standards which "reflect the best scholarship of the last two generations" (Nash, 1998). The need for the standards might be illustrated by the fact that textbooks give more attention to Marilyn Monroe than James Monroe and that United States postal customers chose a stamp of video games over a stamp of the collapse of the Berlin Wall to symbolize the 1980s.

History and Elementary Social Studies

History has long been dominant in the elementary social studies curriculum, while geography also receives a significant emphasis. Together history and geography provide the context or framework of time and place within which the social sciences are studied. History has been understood and addressed in the curriculum in a number of ways: a) as the main subject matter of social studies, often viewed as synonymous with social studies (history-centered curriculum); b) as one of many social science disciplines which are integrated into citizenship education (social sciences integrated curriculum); c) and as closely connected with a literature-based social studies (literature-centered curriculum).

History often entails the study of political science, economics, sociology, and other disciplines of social studies. Historians previously emphasized the political sphere of human activity (heroes and military history, for example) to the exclusion of a more comprehensive history. In recent decades, they have emphasized a wider representation of people (i.e., women's history, Black history, Asian history, etc.) and the history of "everyday life," including the histories of specific communities. This lends support to the idea of integrating the social studies around history.

Historical accounts are sometimes limited to traditional perspectives for the purposes of socialization and the acceptance of particular American values. However, history is also used to address and respond to social problems and policy issues. Both the educational goals of cultural transmission and social criticism are necessary if citizens are to wisely assess the needs for continuity and change in society. However, caution must be taken not to distort history or to engage in a proselytizing effort. Rather, the principles of critical thinking should guide the study of history.

Standards in Historical Thinking

Habits of historical thinking and the engagement of historical empathy (viewing history from the perspectives of those who experienced it) contribute not only to children's historical understanding, but also to their own sense of self and their sense of belonging to the larger community, nation, and world. Historical thinking and historical content cannot be separated in the curriculum, because both the creation and interpretation of history involve the analysis and construction of meaning.

Definitions of history attest to this dynamic process. For example: History is principled and humanistic dialogue between us and our ancestors . . . [it] is the reconstruction of past events, through a dialogue between surviving evidence about the past and existing analytical, theoretical, and political concerns in the present (Florencia Mallon quoted in Leinhardt, Beck, & Stainton, 1994, p. 216).

History is a discipline that is framed by chronology and geography but it is not constrained or limited by them. It is not a collection of reminiscences or anecdotal chit-chat any more than it is a list of vacuous dates. Thinking in history means being literate within these frames and being capable of analysis, synthesis, and case building. To achieve these goals, students need to have both opportunities to reason in history and guidance from history teachers who are able to think flexibly, dynamically, and powerfully within their discipline (Leinhardt, Beck, & Stainton, 1994, p. 254).

The National Center for History in the Schools developed standards of historical thinking (1996) that include these broad categories:
1) Chronological Thinking
2) Historical Comprehension
3) Historical Analysis and Interpretation
4) Historical Research Capabilities
5) Historical Issues-Analysis and Decision-Making

Specific skills are detailed in each of these categories for two levels, K-Grade 4 and Grades 5+. The skills, which average 35 in number, are almost identical. The upper grade skills predictably include more abstract and complex components.

Chronological Thinking

Aspects of time addressed by the standards in this category are time as past, present, and future; timeline representations; change and continuity; and for the upper grades, historical succession, duration, and periodization.

Chronological thinking in terms of specific dates and historical periods is not a prerequisite for learning history in the primary grades. In fact, dates, rather than aiding the development of understanding chronological time, are generally confusing to children (Barton & Levstik, 1996). Likewise, it is not necessary for children to learn clock time or calendar time prior to learning and using historical chronology.

Initially, children conceive of historical time as long ago and now (K-grade 1). Their understanding becomes more complex as they expand the categories of time into long ago and longer ago, now and close to now, and another period of time identified as midway between the original now and long ago (grades 2-3). By third grade children can understand the mathematical basis for dates, but do not use them in an historical sense until about fifth grade. They begin to conceive of decades and centuries (grade 3) and later, of specific historic events connected with specific dates and years. Their understandings of historical periods, prior to formal study in history in fifth grade, are linked with popular culture (e.g., *Happy Days, Little House on the Prairie*) or meaningful period-related concepts (e.g., at the time of the Revolution, or at the time of Columbus) (grades 3-4). Only later do they use the adult terms for time periods which have been identified by historians.

Historical Comprehension

Historical comprehension draws upon understandings of historical time, so that students are able to "depict a person, place, artifact or event in the past using some form of time language" (Thornton & Vukelich, 1988, cited by Barton & Levstik, 1996, p.421). Historical comprehension involves the identification of document sources, their explicit meaning, and the key questions they address. Comprehension skills also extend to the use of data from maps, graphs, and a wide variety of visuals. Historical perspectives are appreciated and engaged in imaginatively. Historical comprehension occurs through narrative and concrete contexts that are meaningful to children. This understanding becomes more complex as children develop and are exposed to the formal study of history.

Primary sources and artifacts frequently used to enhance children's historical comprehension include photos, diaries and journals, letters and family records, interviews and oral histories, newspapers, and other artifacts from the material cultures of the students' families or from museums and historic sites. Through these materials, students see "what things looked like, what people did, and how they did it" (Barton & Levstik, 1996, p. 443).

Narrative sources including historical fiction, non-fiction, and myths and legends are also used to bring history to life.

Historical comprehension further involves correcting misinformation and misconceptions, building upon children's existing knowledge, utilizing interdisciplinary concepts (the concepts of history are interdisciplinary in nature), constructing one's own concepts (constructivist learning), and focusing on much more than correct factual answers.

Historical Analysis and Interpretation

As students engage in historical analysis, they must be concerned with the accuracy of sources and the justification for historical conclusions. A completely objective representation of the past is not possible. The selection of information is affected by the perspectives of whoever is selecting the data. Howard Zinn (1997) cautions citizens that the most important question you [can] ask about anything, any set of historical facts presented to you, is not so much "Is this a false fact?" or "Is it a true fact?" The most important question you can ask is, "What has been left out? What hasn't been told to me?"

Howard Zinn's book, *A People's History,* is a testimony to this important observation as he unravels the broader narratives of American history. Other important examples are Ronald Takaki's *A Different Mirror,* addressing previously omitted portions of America's multicultural history, and Eric Foner's *The New American History.*

Historical analysis and interpretation skill standards require the ability to question our own judgments, to hold a point of view tentatively, and to understand multiple points of view, ideas, values, and so on. The skills of recognizing cause and effect relationships, analyzing multiple causes for events, determining the effects of the past, and understanding the idea that people can influence historical events are also key components of analysis and interpretation.

Historical Research Capabilities

Recent attention to developing skills in students as historians has resulted in many innovative history projects (see Pleasant Company's *America at School* program, 1-800-233-0264; the Teacher's Curriculum Institute *History Alive* program, 1-800-497-6138; and the Westridge Young Writer's Project, *Kids Explore America's Heritage,* 1-800-888-7504). Students-as-historians demonstrate the historical research capabilities of seeking out and assessing data and presenting and supporting their findings.

The research process delineated by these standards may necessitate the learning of interviewing, letter-writing, computer research, and other skills.

Sources for the research often extend beyond the classroom to historic sites or other locations which hold community records, communication on the internet, and analysis of one's own family history. Gaps in historical records, difficulties accessing records, and other aspects of "real world" historical inquiry raise important issues about historical interpretation.

Since topics of inquiry may be generated by students, the learning process can contribute to their development as self-directed learners and independent thinkers. Student-initiated inquiry may also contribute to their personal and social development.

Historical Issues-Analysis and Decision-Making

This standard is about applying historical research skills in the context of historical and present-day dilemmas--history in the service of citizenship. Decision-making and issues analysis are value-laden processes. In *Declarations of Independence,* Howard Zinn writes of his own value orientation toward the study of history:

> For me, history could only be a way of understanding and helping to change . . . what was wrong in the world. . . It meant asking questions that were important for social change, questions relating to equality, liberty, peace, and justice, but being open to whatever answers were suggested by looking at history...I decided early that I would be biased in the sense of holding fast to certain fundamental values: the equal right of all human beings--whatever race, nationality, sex, religion--to life, liberty and the pursuit of happiness, Jefferson's ideals. It seemed to me that devoting a life to the study of history was worthwhile only if it aimed at those ideals (1990, p. 48-49).

Furthering democracy is one central outcome of the standards of historical thinking as they are coupled with action. Key questions are asked as issues are analyzed--"Whose interests are served by a particular course of action? What values underlie particular points of view? Are certain courses of action ethical or just? What alternatives might better serve democracy?" Questions such as these are brought to historical study in the standards which follow, and action can be taken in response to what is learned.

Overview of Standards in History for Grades K-4

Topic 1: Living and Working Together in Families and Communities, Now and Long Ago.

> Standard 1: Family life now and in the recent past. Family life in various places long ago.
>
> Standard 2: History of students' local community and how communities in North America varied long ago.

Topic 2: The History of the Students' Own State or Region.

> Standard 3: The people, events, problems, and ideas that created the history of their state.

Topic 3: The History of the United States: Democratic Principles and Values and the Peoples from Many Cultures Who Contributed to Its Cultural, Economic and Political Heritage

> Standard 4: How democratic values came to be, and how they have been exemplified by people, events, and symbols.
>
> Standard 5: The causes and nature of various movements of large groups of people into and within the united states, now and long ago.
>
> Standard 6: Regional folklore and cultural contributions that helped to form our national heritage.

Topic 4: The History of Peoples of Many Cultures Around the World.

> Standard 7: Selected attributes and historical developments of various societies in Africa, the Americas, Asia, and Europe.
>
> Standard 8: Major discoveries in science and technology, their social and economic effects, and the scientists and inventors responsible for them.

(National Center for History in the Schools, 1996, p. 25)

Standards in History for Grades K-4

The "Overview of Standards in History for Grades K-4" integrates the standards for historical thinking with the standards for historical understanding. This outline of topics is adaptable to several common curricular patterns--a modified "expanding environments" approach (the traditional social studies pattern of studying the self-family-neighborhood-community-state-nation, and then the world), bringing in historical perspectives throughout; the history-centered California framework focusing on here, there, and then (integrating the distant and the past with the students' present experience and context); and also a literature and history emphasis (rich history through a literature-based curriculum).

Four topics organize these standards: 1) family and community; 2) state or region; 3) nation; 4) world. The eight standards provided within the four topics can be addressed at any and all of the grade levels, K-4. While the topics appear to reproduce an expanding environments sequence, the grade levels suggested span grades K-4 and are not limited to a single grade level. Also notable is the increased amount of history content beyond what is usually integrated into the curriculum at these earlier grade levels. Primary grade social studies has been criticized for presenting little if any history content, and covering much of what students already know, and these standards address that criticism:

> The standards for historical understanding, grades K-4, define what the students should know about the history of families, their communities, states, nation, and world. These understandings are drawn from the record of human aspirations, strivings, accomplishments, and failures in at least five spheres of human activity: the social, political, scientific/technological, economic, and cultural (the philosophical/religious/aesthetic), as appropriate for children (National Center for History in the Schools, 1996, p. 2).

Standards one and two address the family and community in terms of understanding the past and how the values and ways of life of diverse groups passed on their unique heritage. The student's own family, culture, and community are studied in a way that personalizes history. The growth of different types of communities; the unique characteristics of Native American tribes, colonial and pioneer communities, and other ethnically diverse groups; and an understanding of how family structures have changed over time highlight these standards.

When studying students' families, students may not know or have access to information about their parentage or ancestry. Due to increasingly complex lifestyles, adoptions, and factors such as the difficulty of researching the history of ancestors who were slaves, it is important to know whether this content is available for a given group of students.

An extensive variety of sources are noted in these standards, from which students interpret and evaluate data. They include the oral tradition and artifacts as cultural communication, which is especially important when written records of a group's history are not available. When slaves, for example, were not allowed to read and write, other forms of communication became the content of their history. *Harriet Powers's Bible Quilts* (Perry, 1994) is one highly regarded example of this. Also, *Dia's Story Cloth, The Hmong People's Journey of Freedom* (Cha, 1996) communicates a people's history through artifacts. These materials allow for a more inclusive history.

Standard three addresses state or regional history and how a particular state's or region's development and identity are unique. Included are what brought settlers to the state, how statehood was gained, key people and events and their relationship to national history, problems and how they were solved, and the influence of geography on the history of the state. A wide variety of sources are specifically highlighted--buildings, statues, monuments, place names, census data, newspapers, magazines, legends, myths, and other data.

Notable aspects of the students' study include the examination of history all the way back to the indigenous peoples of the region, the comparison of these groups in the past with their lives today, the study of other groups who settled in the area, and the interrelationships between these groups. The "sources of strength and determination" used by various groups to overcome problems such as prejudice and intolerance (i.e., family, community, church, synagogue, etc.) is another key component of this standard.

Standards four through six, concerning the history of the United States, present a balance between the ideals and realities of our "democracy." They address the development of democracy, the principles of democracy set out in the Declaration of Independence, and the basic rights guaranteed by the Constitution and the Bill of Rights. The diverse cultural heritage of this nation of immigrants encompasses many regions of the country and movements across the country throughout its history.

Historic figures, commemorations, and national symbols are selected as important aspects of our heritage. The Pledge of Allegiance and patriotic songs and poems are also included. Holidays selected for study are said to "celebrate and exemplify fundamental values and principles of American democracy" (National Center for History in the Schools, 1996, p. 33).

Presumably, Columbus Day is not listed among the holidays because of a sensitivity to its multiple interpretations. "The forced relocation of Native Americans and how their lives, rights, and territories were affected by

European colonization and the expansion of the United States" (National Center for History in the Schools, 1996, p. 34), is presented in the standards, after which examples, such as the Cherokee Trail of Tears is provided.

The standards do not attempt to identify every event or example of content that might be covered in United States History. But it would be consistent with the standards to address such topics as the Native American contributions to our political heritage (Johansen, 1982), and the history of intolerance in our country (Guggenheim, 1995), regrettably an important lesson for our young people to learn and overcome. Examples of intolerance might include the internment of the Japanese Americans and how the United States admitted its wrongdoing. The standards do address "the opportunities and obstacles [the immigrants] encountered when they arrived in America" (Guggenheim, 1995). These failures accompanied the growth of the nation.

The 200-year struggle to achieve what is promised by our democracy and the ordinary and extraordinary people who have courageously fought for the common good are important components of the standards. "The role of protest in a democracy" (Guggenheim, 1995, p. 34), including protest songs and symbols, is noted and lends balance to the standards.

Standards seven and eight extend the context of history to the world. The development of societies in Africa, the Americas, Asia, and Europe is addressed in standard seven, and discoveries and inventions and their influence on society is addressed in standard eight. Peoples in various cultures and times are studied in terms of their community and family life, cultural characteristics and traditions (i.e., customs, arts, myths and legends, etc.), and achievements.

The history of peoples without written records and the influences of geography on developing societies provide a foundation for the study of exploration and world travel, and the consequences of these journeys. Migrations of large groups of people from ancient to recent times are also included.

The development of early societies (i.e., hunters and gatherers, farmers, etc.) as they first used inventions such as the wheel and basic tools, and as they learned to control the elements and use natural resources leads to 19th Century inventions and their influence on society. Various types of developments in transportation and communication are detailed in the standards. The inventors and scientists behind these achievements are noted as well. The positive and negative effects of technological development and the ethical issues raised by various inventions and discoveries are important points which are raised again in the following standards.

Social Studies Content for the Elementary School Teacher p. 10

Eras Covered by the United States History Standards

Era 1: Three Worlds Meet (Beginnings to 1620)
Era 2: Colonization and Settlement (1585-1763)
Era 3: Revolution and the New Nation (1754-1820s)
Era 4: Expansion and Reform (1801-1861)
Era 5: Civil War and Reconstruction (1850-1877)
Era 6: The Development of the Industrial United States (1870-1900)
Era 7: The Emergence of Modern America (1890-1930)
Era 8: The Great Depression and World War II (1929-1945)
Era 9: Postwar United States (1945 to early 1970s)
Era 10: Contemporary United States (1968 to the present)

Eras Covered by the World History Standards

Era 1: The Beginnings of Human Society
Era 2: Early Civilizations and the Emergence of Pastoral Peoples, 4000-1000 BCE
Era 3: Classical Traditions, Major Religions, and Giant Empires, 1000 BCE-300 CE
Era 4: Expanding Zones of Exchange and Encounter, 300-1000 CE
Era 5: Intensified Hemispheric Interactions, 1000-1500 CE
Era 6: The Emergence of the First Global Age, 1450-1770
Era 7: An Age of Revolutions, 1750-1914
Era 8: A Half-Century of Crisis and Achievement, 1900-1945
Era 9: The 20th Century Since 1945: Promises and Paradoxes
World History Across the Eras

The United States and World History Standards

The United States History Standards consist of 31 standards covering 10 eras of American history. The World History Standards consist of 46 standards covering 9 eras of world history with an additional overview of "World History Across the Eras" (addressing "long-term changes and recurring patterns in world history"). The number of standards for each era varies. In addition, they contain detailed standards' components and numerous "extended standards," examples of what students will know at particular grade levels.

The content of United States and World History covered in grades 5 and 6 varies significantly with state and local curriculum requirements. Traditionally fifth grade is devoted to United States History, and somewhere between sixth and eighth grades, World History is presented. The standards intend that 3 years each be devoted to United States and World History somewhere between grades 5 and 12.

A comprehensive treatment of United States History gives space to recent history, the history of people's movements, the history of ordinary people as well as elite, class history, women's history, religious history, and so on. A balanced history also discusses the consequences and implications of negative information about the United States, and other countries.

World History provides an understanding of diverse civilizations and cultures in the past and present. It also provides the larger context for the interrelated national, state, and local histories. The events of history should be presented in the widest possible geographic and social context. For example, slavery is best understood in the larger context of the Caribbean and Western Africa.

The world history standards do not attempt to cover the histories of all people and traditions, but to "identify those developments in the past that involved and affected relatively large numbers of people and that had broad significance" (Ibid., p. 45). A closer look at the standards' content of United States and World History for grades 5 and 6 follows.

United States History Content Standards

Three Worlds Meet

The first era focuses on interactions between the Americas, Western Europe, and Western Africa during the period of European exploration, colonization, and conquest. The political, social, economic, religious, and geographic aspects of societies in these areas of the world contextualize the catastrophic losses of Native American lives, the enslavement of Africans, and the cultural influences of diverse peoples in the developing America. Cultural perspectives (i.e., Europeans, Natives, and Africans) of the explorers' travels, the accuracy of accounts related to the "discovery of America," and the origins of Native Americans some 30,000 or more years ago are addressed.

Colonization and Settlement

The Colonial Period, covering nearly two centuries, builds the foundations for our political, economic, religious, social, and cultural institutions. Slavery influenced economic institutions and values; Puritanism influenced religion; and the idea of representative government (i.e., the House of Burgesses) influenced politics. The diversity of groups involved in the European colonization and settlement, including free and indentured immigrants (hundreds of thousands, ultimately several million) and involuntary immigrants or enslaved Africans (ultimately 10-12 million or more), directly contributed to these institutions. The colonies' distinctive characteristics and institutional practices also reflect this diversity (e.g., economic regions, governments, family and community life, and religious practices, etc.).

Enlightenment ideas and experiments with electricity are some high points of the period. Violent relationships with indigenous peoples, loss of Native American land, African slave trade, and the development of a slave labor system are among the tragedies. The irony of religious intolerance being practiced by those who came to America for their own religious freedom is also an important aspect of life in the colonies.

Revolution and the New Nation

Events leading to the Revolution (e.g., the French and Indian War and other battles, the Treaty of Paris, and taxes imposed on the colonists by the British, etc.), the events of the Revolution (including the role of George Washington and the contributions of other countries to the war effort), and the consequences of the Revolution (e.g., the economic and political factors that led to Shay's Rebellion, the institutions created by the new nation, the development of the government through debate over the Articles of Confederation, the calling of the Constitutional Convention, and the emerging two-party system) frame the study of this period.

Beliefs about the causes of the war vary from the traditional view of American colonists fighting for their rights and liberties to the view of the war and resulting constitution as actions of protecting class interests (see Davis, 1990; Zinn, 1997). Views of the war from differing perspectives: urban and rural, slave and free, male and female, native and colonizer, differing classes, and differing religious and ideological beliefs all contribute to understanding this period of history. The perspectives of ordinary people are addressed by Young, Fife, and Janzen (1993) through documents and artifacts.

The basic principles of our democratic government as expressed in the Declaration of Independence and the Constitution, the origins of these ideas, their significance in their own time, and their enduring influence are of central importance here. However, they were only a beginning. The constitution was, according to Thurgood Marshall:

> defective from the start, requiring several amendments, a civil war, and momentous social transformation to attain the system of constitutional government and its respect for individual freedoms and human rights, we hold as fundamental today (Marshall, 1987, cited by Young, Fife, & Janzen, 1993, p. xv).

Views of various icons emerging in this period should also be accurately assessed (see the PBS American Experience video on George Washington).

Expansion and Reform

The period defined as the new nation prior to the Civil War covers many major developments. Land expansion and the settlement of the West, the removal and resettlement of Native Americans, the expansion of slavery, increasing immigration, the industrial revolution, and changing foreign relations are some of these.

The idea of Manifest Destiny, that the United States was a "chosen" nation, whose destiny was to inhabit the continent, seemed to be confirmed by the land acquisitions of this period (e.g., the Louisiana Purchase, California and the Southwest in the Mexican-American War, the annexation of Texas, and the removal of Native American tribes).

The Oregon boundary dispute was resolved, and California and Oregon were rapidly settled. The population had grown from about 4 million in 1790 to 31 million in 1860. Life in the West, immigrant life, slave plantation life, and life in the cities and factories are important aspects of this period.

Technology, reform movements (including the activities of women), and political changes were also influencing the nation. Debates over equality continued, even as contradictions in the suffrage movement and failures to meet treaty obligations occurred. The slavery issue was addressed in the Missouri Compromise, and the Monroe Doctrine stated opposition to foreign interference. Popular participation in presidential elections marked a new political order, and Jackson's administration was said to be a victory for the "Common Man," (meaning men, not women's rights). Jackson's record with the slaves and Indians, however, is not a proud legacy (David, 1990, pp. 120-123).

Civil War and Reconstruction

This period addresses the causes of the Civil War (i.e., slavery, state's rights, and competing visions of the United States, etc.), the course and nature of the war, fundamental constitutional revisions (i.e., the 13th, 14th, and 15th Amendments), and political proclamations and programs related to the war and reconstruction (e.g., the Emancipation Proclamation, The Freedmen's Bureau, and "Black Reconstruction").

Those who died over the four years of the war numbered 620,000 (360,000 Union and over 260,000 Confederate). This number is more than the number of those who died in all other American wars combined. The population of the North was 23 million and the South about 9 million (3.5 million were slaves). One quarter of all Southern men died in the war. Another quarter were crippled by the war. Blacks who fought in the Union numbered 85,000. They were led by whites in segregated units. Union forces outnumbered the South by two to one during most of the war. The South experienced physical devastation, and the loss of the large numbers of men impacted the gender balance nationwide.

Wartime human and material costs, technology, leadership, women's roles, key points in the war, and post-war corruption are topics addressed by the standards, as well as the debates over reconstruction. While radical reconstruction, "the first attempt at establishing biracial democracy," (Ibid., p. 99) failed, and blacks did not receive equal treatment after the war (citizenship came with the 14th Amendment in 1866 and the right to vote with the 15th Amendment in 1870), progress was being made in this direction. Slavery had ended (with the 13th Amendment), and the nation had survived.

The Development of the Industrial United States

By the beginning of the 20th Century, the United States had become an industrial empire. Land, inventions, and laborers contributed to this industrial transformation.

Unprecedented immigration increased the United States population from about 31 million in 1860 to 76 million in 1900. Some 70,000 Chinese alone came to build the transcontinental railroad. New immigrant groups increased the overall diversity of the United States. The settlement patterns and the opportunities, challenges, and contributions of these groups are studied in this period. As urbanization continued, regional geographic characteristics and different types of industries put their mark on the development of the cities.

Farming, mining, and ranching played a significant role in the economy. The environmental costs of the misuse of natural resources became an issue of importance. Technology brought changes to business and industry as well as life in homes and at work. Interestingly, over 640,000 patents were granted between 1865 and 1900.

This era of change highlights prominent industrial and financial leaders along with the emerging labor movement; child labor practices and opposition to them; the "second great removal" of Native Americans along with the breaching of promises by the government (that of a "permanent Indian frontier"); and racial intolerance, conflict, and lynching in the South.

Industrial development came at a cost. The United States army was at war with Indian tribes to gain their land for a continuous 25-year period (1866-1891). The number of children working increased by about 130% in the 30 years prior to 1900. And big business grew from monopolies, cheap labor, and government subsidies. Millions of acres of free land were given to the railroad. Subsidies took many forms and were often gained by corrupt means. The election of 1896 meant defeat for farmers and laborers in their struggle against big business and its domination of government. The issue of imperialism was also raised in the context of the Spanish-American War and the new territories acquired.

The Emergence of Modern America

Progressive reform was needed to address the problems created by industrial capitalism, urbanization, and political corruption. The social and moral ideals of the Progressive Movement are evident in the resulting 16th, 17th, 18th, and 19th Amendments. Presidential support or failure to support reforms and alternative perspectives and proposals for reform (i.e., African American, women, etc.) are significant here.

The role of the United States in the world and World War I and how it developed are additional components of the standards for this era. The United States positions on open and equal trade, restrictive and closed immigration, neutrality in the war, and later involvement in the war (e.g., American Expeditionary Force) are key points. President Wilson's Peace Plan ("Fourteen Points"), the League of Nations, and the Treaty of Versailles are also highlighted.

Characteristics of the United States during this period include the adaptation of the principles of scientific management and new technology to business and the cultural developments of a new mass media culture, the

Harlem Renaissance, and new leisure and entertainment activities. The period is marked by a wide range of concerns within the United States and across the world.

The Great Depression and World War II

The Great Depression and World War II are addressed in terms of their causes and effects. Topics connected with the Great Depression are the stock market crash of 1929, the Dust Bowl, New Deal legislation, and presidential leadership related to the New Deal. The depression profoundly impacted ordinary Americans and influenced the nature of government legislation toward economic relief measures (e.g., farmer's income, old age security, unemployment compensation, and labor rights, etc.). It was only by 1944 that full employment was regained (a 1% unemployment rate in comparison with a high of 25% in 1932).

The study of World War II entails the effects of American isolationism on international relations; the American response to aggression in Europe, Africa, and Asia; the key events of the war in both Europe and the Pacific; the economic and human costs and consequences for the Allies and Axis powers; and the war on the homefront (i.e., United States mobilization of resources, and the internment of Japanese Americans as a denial of civil liberties).

While the United States History standards do not include content about the holocaust or nuclear weapons until grade 7, this content does fit naturally with the big picture of the era provided by the standards. Study of the holocaust may be a state or local curriculum requirement even before fifth grade.

PostWar United States

The Cold War provides the political context for the 45 years following World War II. International conflicts continued with the Korean and VietNam Wars. These conflicts, uprisings in the communist governments of Eastern Europe, and the Arab-Israeli crisis influenced United States foreign policy. United Nations involvement in reducing international conflict is also noted.

Domestic policies highlighted are Truman's civil rights policies, Kennedy's "New Frontier," and Johnson's "Great Society." Under Truman, segregation in the armed forces ended, preparing the way for the Brown v. The Board of Education of Topeka decision, which overturned the constitutionality of "Separate But Equal" practices. Johnson's reform program was the most extensive social and economic legislation since the New Deal. Racial segregation and discrimination in employment became illegal and federal aid for education, health care, and numerous other legislation supported the "war on poverty." Johnson enacted much of Kennedy's "New Frontier" legislation, which extended the New Deal's social reform agenda. These were permanent changes which proved challenging to implement effectively.

Social changes occurred as many diverse groups sought their civil rights and equal opportunity, but not without opposition from the South and conflict over women's issues (i.e., the Equal Rights Amendment and Roe v. Wade). A Supreme Court decision was also made concerning freedom of religion.

Economic strength was evident in a growing consumer culture, the GI Bill supported education, women made up one-third of the nation's workforce (by 1960, 40% of the women were employed), research led to the discovery of DNA, and developing technology supported the space program.

Contemporary United States

The social, political, scientific/technological, economic, and cultural spheres of human activity once again organize the key events and perspectives of the era. The technology revolution transforms the economy, the workplace, and the home. A new wave of immigration (4 million in the 1970s) continues to impact the United States and its religious diversity in particular. The development of the women's movement and women's organizations establish it as an important force for equality. The increasing popularity of sports influences American culture, as do international entertainment and the arts. The influence of the media on culture can be felt by all ages, although the standards so not identify it for study in grades 5 or 6. A multitude of issues are included: economic and environmental issues addressed by the Nixon, Ford, and Carter administrations; the scandal of Watergate during Nixon's administration (astronauts also landed on the moon); and Reagan's strengthening of the military and reducing federal spending on welfare. Issues and events such as, the collapse of communist governments and politics after the Cold War, Gay liberation, affirmative action, and so forth, are addressed in later grades. The selection of content for the contemporary period is more difficult because it involves interpreting current history without the benefit of assessing its long-term significance.

World History Content Standards

[The World History Standards] encourage students to ask large and searching questions about the human past, to compare patterns of continuity and change in different parts of the world, and to examine the histories and achievements of particular peoples or civilizations with an eye to wider social, cultural, or economic contexts (National Center for History in the Schools, pp. 45-46).

The Beginnings of Human Society

Archaeological evidence places the earliest humans in Africa. Hunter-gather and farming communities are contrasted, and human interactions with varied environments (e.g., Africa, Americas, and Western Eurasia) are compared.

Early Civilizations and the Emergence of Pastoral Peoples

Early civilizations occurred mostly in river valleys. These civilizations had developed agriculture and were characterized as agricultural, pastoral (herding and using animals as a primary food source), and urban. They emerged at different times in different places: northern Middle East (Mesopotamia) at about 3500 BCE, Egypt at about 3000 BCE, China from 1500 BCE, and Central America (Olmecs) from 800 BCE. The early Indian civilization along the Indus River did not survive invasions (after 2 millennia).

Forms of societal organization (e.g., pastoral kinship, agrarian society, etc.) and technology varied (e.g., chariots for transport and warfare, plow and bronze-making technology), as did their interactions with the environment. Communication (the emergence of writing), trade, population growth, and the spread of agriculture led to developments in the Classical Period. Reasons for the decline of civilization and ways that groups assimilate and adapt cultural characteristics are important aspects of this period.

Classical Traditions, Major Religions, and Giant Empires

This period of classical civilizations exemplifies the development of new economic, political, social, religious, and cultural forms in Southwest Asia/Eurasia, Africa, India, China, and the Mediterranean region. The emerging agrarian civilization in Mesoamerica and factors in its development are also noted (i.e., maize cultivation and Olmec contributions), as are the pastoral nomadic peoples of Central Asia.

The emergence of Judaism, Christianity, Hinduism, Buddhism, Confucianism, and Daoism, as well as the beginnings of their long-term influences are significant in this era. The development of Greek city-states, Athenian democracy in contrast with Sparta's military aristocracy, the development of the Roman Republic and Empire, and slavery or forced labor in Greece, Rome, China, and India are also highlighted.

Trade (i.e., with Phoenicians, in the Nile valley, and trans-Eurasian "silk roads"); war, military conquest, and empire unification (i.e., wars between Persia and Greek city-states, Alexander the Great's conquests, and unification in the Chinese empire); and cultural development (i.e., Hellenic architecture, sculpture, and painting) are recurring themes.

This era saw river valley civilizations develop into major empires, which remained until the invasions from 300-600 CE.

Expanding Zones of Exchange and Encounter

The "postclassical" period begins with the decline of the Roman Empire, the Han Empire (China), and the Gupta Empire (India). While these civilizations undergo substantive change, some continuity with previous societal patterns is observable. China experiences several centuries of disruption; Indian civilization no longer generates large empires; and the Mediterranean is divided with Greco-Roman traditions remaining only in the Byzantine Empire. Belief systems continue their influence: Hinduism and Buddhism on India and Southeast Asia; and Christianity, Buddhism, and Islam across Afro-Eurasia.

Societal developments include the Tang dynasty and its diverse population in China, indigenous development and the emperor state in Japan, and the Maya society and culture in Mesoamerica. New European states replace the Roman Empire and various Christian orders emerge (i.e., the Latin Church, monasteries, convents, etc.). Migrations and invasions cause change in Europe and Oceania, and connections between societies are observable through trade routes and religious conversion.

Intensified Hemispheric Interactions

In this era, the entire Eastern Hemisphere became an interconnected region with its own history. Growth in Europe and China made this possible. China became the largest world economy through technological innovation and expansion of trade across land and sea. Europe was redefined in this period through feudalism, monarchies, city-states, and military power (i.e., the European Crusades, Christian opposition to Muslim power, etc.). Medieval legal and educational European institutions influenced the formation of their modern counterparts.

The period is also noted for the rise and fall of the Mongol Empire, the largest land empire in global history, which lasted less than 100 years. Feudalism and a warrior culture developed in Japan and Southeast Asia, and the Aztec and Inca empires developed in the Americas. Islamic cultural and scientific development and the expansion of Muslim communities across the central two-thirds of Afro-Eurasia, coincided with state, town, and trade developments in Sub-Saharan Africa. European economic changes, cultural developments, the Hundred Years War, and the plague of the Black Death are also noted. Empires vying for power in Eastern Europe and the Near East were the Ottoman Empire and the Byzantine Empire, which fell to the Turks at Constantinople, at the beginning of the Global Age.

The Emergence of the First Global Age

Western Europe became more prominent in world history at this time. European states were aggressively competitive in commerce and colonization. They sought gold to exchange for Asian goods and used Asian inventions (e.g., explosive powder, compass, etc.) along with their own inventions (i.e., shipbuilding, navigation, etc.) in exploration and trade. Western Europeans sought direct contact with Asia apart from Muslim intermediaries.

Europeans made connections with Sub-Saharan Africa, Asia, and the Americas, which led to expansion and exchange (including plants and animals, and the crops of sugar and tobacco), but also political and military conflict (i.e., between the Spanish and the Aztec and Inca Empires). European society was undergoing institutional changes; the Renaissance; the Reformation; the English Revolution; the Scientific Revolution (i.e., Copernicus to Newton); and the Enlightenment. At the same time, it organized and financed the slave trade.

China's Ming Dynasty; the unification of Persia; the Mughal conquest of India; Japan's shogunate; the success of the Ottoman Empire; and the political, commercial, and naval activity of England, France, and the Netherlands are also significant to this period.

An Age of Revolutions

In the previous era, Europe became more prominent on the global scene. In this period, Europeans dominated the world's land, 35% in 1800 and 84% in 1914. European influence on the world was profound, although its land domination was short-lived.

Political, industrial, and communication revolutions and related inventions also mark this period. Revolutions, rebellion, and independence movements in the United States, France, Haiti, South America, and Latin America and the democratic and nationalist ideas that influenced them are a major focus of this period. The agricultural and industrial revolutions in England, the expansion of industrial economies in Europe and the Atlantic basin, and the suppression of trans-Atlantic trade in the context of movements against slavery are also key themes.

Eurasian societies were transformed by the invasion of France, the unification of Germany and Italy, Russian expansion, the British conquest of India, Japan's Meji State and movement from shogunates to states, Japan's industrial and technological development, and China's resistance to European contact in politics and trade. In Africa, the Zulu Empire, the discovery of diamonds and gold, and changes in political geography also held significance for Western dominance.

A Half-Century of Crisis and Achievement

World history in the first half of the 20th Century includes revolution and social change (i.e., the Mexican Revolution, industrial development in Europe, Japan, and the United States, etc.), World Wars I and II (including their causes, consequences, key leaders, and events), and the 1920s and 1930s' search for stability in between.

This era saw major changes in world geopolitics and the United States role internationally. New technologies benefited humanity and put humanity at risk. Massive industrial production and military technology greatly influenced the "unprecedented violence and destruction" of the wars.

Events in Russia (i.e., the Russian Revolution of 1917, Joseph Stalin's rise to power, etc.); the conference at Versailles and the League of Nations; changes in European colonial rule in Africa and the Middle East; pan-Arabism and nationalist Middle East struggles; consequences of the Great Depression in the United States; German, Italian, and Japanese military activities; fascist and Nazi regimes and their consequences (supremely, the inhumane "devastation suffered by the Jews"); and of course, social and cultural changes (i.e., the rise of a world mass media culture; the influence of the automobile, airplane, and railway on world commerce, global migration, and lifestyle; etc.) mark this era.

The 20th Century Since 1945: Promises and Paradoxes

This era begins at the end of World War II. Connections to the past are made as United States' positions and leadership roles after World War I and World War II are contrasted, and as factors that led to the Cold War are explored. International conflicts, many of which are related to the Cold War, continue, and the United Nations is founded. Massive decolonization occurs and the number of new nations increases even more as the Soviet Union is dissolved and revolutions in Eastern Europe divide other nations.

The declining economic, political, and military dominance of the West occurs as international contact is intensified through new forms of global communication, trade, and interdependence. The global economy continues to develop (i.e., the Pacific Rim economy, the European Economic Community, etc.), as global industrialization, an unprecedented growth in population, and massive migrations characterize the contemporary period. Persistent problems of poverty, environmental degradation, and issues concerning advancements in science and technology continue to be important.

Sustained efforts are made by international, government, political, citizen, and special interest groups to address human and civil rights on a worldwide scale (e.g., progress in women's rights, the end of Apartheid in South Africa, etc.). The spread of democracy and the developing global culture reflect the continuing influence of the West.

World History Across the Eras

The concluding standard focuses on identifying patterns across the eras of World History. What have been the results of human activity in the spheres of social, political, scientific/technological, economic, and cultural (the philosophical/religious/ aesthetic) life? What have been the results of human activity in relationship to the natural environment and other peoples? Examples are listed: the development of cities, trade, ideals and institutions, the practice of slavery, and the use of the environment.

The enduring issues of humanity span nations and times The questions of "What is next? What has not worked, and how can we improve our societies and civilizations?" lead to innovations which build upon the past. New ways of sharing a common space, resources, and opportunities can be conceptualized.

Reflections and Conclusions

History is an ongoing and imperfect process of interpreting events and passing on our historical understandings to new generations, as the centuries unfold. It is a process of revealing answers to questions, and examining the historical data beneath the surface of images masquerading as reality. Accurately interpreted history is illusive. We cannot expect a history without paradoxes or answers without questions. But we can be inspired by individuals of character and courage, by democratic ideals, and by the possibility of shaping events, at least as much as we are shaped by them.

References

Barton, K. C., & Levstik. L. S. (1996). "Back when God was around and everything": Elementary children's understanding of historical time. *American Educational Research Journal, 33*(2), 419-454.

Cha, D. (1996). *Dia's story cloth: The Hmong people's journey of freedom.* New York: Lee & Low.

Davis, K. C. (1990). *Don't know much about history: Everything you need to know about American history but never learned.* New York: Crown.

Foner, E. (1990). *The New American History.* Philadelphia: Temple University Press.

Guggenheim, C. (Producer). (1995). *The shadow of hate: A history of intolerance in America.* Montgomery, AL: Teaching Tolerance.

Johansen, B. E. (1982). *Forgotten fathers: How the American Indian helped shape democracy.* Boston: The Harvard Common Press.

Leinhardt, G., Beck, I. L., & Stainton, C. (Eds.). (1994). *Teaching and learning in history.* Hillsdale, NJ: Lawrence Erlbaum.

Nash, G. (1998). National History Standards [Video, No. 100422]. Washington, DC: C-SPAN.

National Center for History in the Schools. (1996). *National standards for history: Basic edition.* Los Angeles, Author.

Perry, R. A. (1994). *Harriet Powers's Bible quilts.* New York: Rizzoli International.

Smith, R. N. (1999). Education: American Presidents Series [Video]. Washington, DC: C-SPAN.

Takaki, R. (1993). *A different mirror: A history of multicultural America.* Boston: Little, Brown.

Young, A. F., & Fife, T. J. with Janzen, M. E. (1993). *We the people: Voices and images of the new nation.* Philadelphia: Temple University Press.

Zinn, H. (1997). Historical interpretation [Video, No. 78710]. Washington, DC: C-SPAN.

Zinn, H. (1995). *A People's history of the United States: 1492-present* (rev. ed.). New York: Harper Perennial. (See also "The Wall Charts" of *A People's History*, published by The New Press.)

Zinn, H. (1990). *Declarations of independence: Cross-examining American ideology.* New York: Harper Collins.

References For Further Understanding

Eck, D. L., & The Pluralism Project, Harvard University. (1997). *On common ground: World religions in America* [CD-ROM]. New York: Columbia University Press. This cutting-edge CD-ROM includes the history of 15 world religions.

Eyewitness history of the world. [CD-ROM]. (1995). New York: Dorling Kindersley. World history is fun to learn with this CD-ROM.

Headings, M. D., Houston, T. (Ed.), & Housley, K. (Ed.). (1997). *Teaching American History with the Internet, Grades K-6 Internet lesson plans and classroom activities.* Lancaster, PA: Classroom Connect. See <www.classroom.net> for more websites and publications.

National Archives and Records Administration, 700 Pennsylvania Ave., NW, Washington, DC 20408; 202-501-5402; <http://www.nara.gov/>. Primary source documents for particular historic eras and topics are available (see also *Teaching with Documents*). Golden Owl, Facts on File, and Perfection Learning publishers also produce quality primary source materials.

Organization of American Historians, 112 N. Bryan St., Bloomington, IN 47408-4199; 812-855-7311. *OAH Magazine of History* provides history related to selected themes and events (see *American Stories,* collected readings on minority history). Organizations devoted to specific groups, such as the National Women's History Project, are also notable.

Perez-Stable, M. A., & Cordier, M. H. (1994). *Understanding American History through children's literature: Instructional units and activities for grades K-8.* Phoenix: Oryx. Introduces children's literature as it relates to eras of American History.

GEOGRAPHY

Dr. Jay Monson
Utah State University

"Where are you from?"
"Where do you live?"
"Where were you born?"
"Where do you work?"

These and many other questions underscore the importance of "place" in our social world. Geography-oriented questions are often used as introductions in our interaction with others. Children, too, have many "natural" interests and curiosities in topics which are part of geography. "What is the highest place on the earth, or the wettest, driest, ... or the largest city, state, nation ... or where did more people cram into a phone booth than any other location!" Needless to say, the *Guinness Book of World Records* is a best seller among children of elementary school age. They also love to collect stamps, coins, sports cards, and artifacts from the world over. These and other "natural interests" lie within the area of geography for K-6 students.

What is Geography?
Geography offers us a framework for studying our world. It enables us to find answers to questions about our planet. Geography literally means "to describe the earth" — "geo" (the earth), "graphy" (to describe). Unlike geology, which deals with studying the solid matter of which the earth is composed--especially it's rocks--geography is centered on people and where and how they live. Geography has two general sub-divisions; physical geography and cultural geography (or "human geography" referred to by some). The latter is the main focal point for the elementary grades. Keeping a "people orientation" is more developmentally appropriate for K-6 learners.
 However, it is important to blend in some physical geography with the cultural emphasis. One cannot study one area without the other. Together they provide understanding of such questions as: Where are we? Where do we want to go? Where have we been? What are the needs of people in various places on this earth? What happens to us when we live in one place versus another?

Physical geography deals with information concerning land forms, bodies of water, climate, weather, and plant and animal life relevant to the study of our activities as people in various settings.

Cultural geography focuses on how we as people *interact* with our physical and cultural environments. Topics include living in selected cultures, historical, demographic (population) facts and figures, urban and rural life, economic, political, and other aspects of our settlement and life on this earth.

Studying comparative relationships between any and all of the above is also appropriate for children in the elementary grades. "Life in extremely cold areas as compared with life in hot, desert areas" is one example. "Where people live influences how they build shelter, acquire food, dress, and work," is another.

Broad concepts of interdependence emerging in local studies and extending through regional and international studies are also appropriate, leading to a key understanding so important in understanding today's world--that of global interdependence.

Globes and Maps

The primary tools of geographers are maps and globes. Instruction about globes and maps is a major contribution of geography to a child's education. Maps are two-dimensional charts that describe the earth, while globes add a very important third dimension. This is sometimes overlooked due to ease of handling paper maps as opposed to having a globe for reference. For young children, however, it is absolutely paramount to have globes available when teaching geography, for *all* flat maps are distorted. Just compare the total land size of Greenland with the USA on any flat map and then on a globe, to see how distortion enters into the picture. It is true that a map of a smaller area, such as a town or city, is more accurate than one of larger areas, but *all flat maps are distorted.* Thus, using a globe creates a much better understanding of size and location and is an important underpinning for life-long understanding of concepts from the area of geography.

The chart on the following page shows some common map symbols. How many do you know? (Answers appear at the top of page 29.)

MAP AND GLOBE SKILLS TO BE DEVELOPED
IN THE ELEMENTARY SCHOOL

1. Use and understand the globe as a model of the earth.
2. Observe systematically, identify, and note the location, distribution and density of features of the landscape.
3. Orient self and note directions in space and in maps and globes.
4. Locate places, distributions, and densities on maps and globes.
5. Use scale to judge or measure distance in space and on maps and globes.
6. Use and understand symbols and visualize the realities for which they stand.
7. Use cartographic principles of map composition and graphic expression.
8. Recognize and express relative location.
9. Use and understand basic map projections.
10. Understand and relate area distributions.

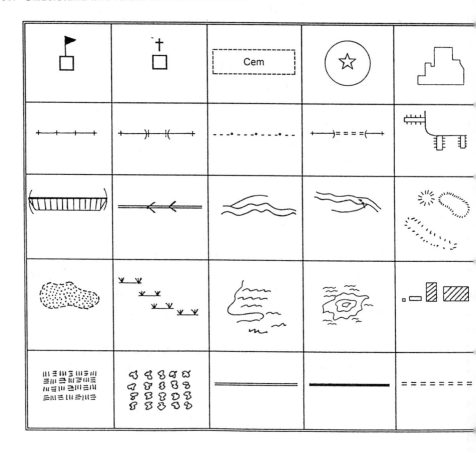

Correct answers for each row (left to right):
school, church, cemetery, capital city, large city boundary
railroad, bridge, power transmission line, tunnel, wharfs or docks
large dam, canal with lock, river and stream, waterfall, mountain range
dry lake, marsh or swamp, peninsula, island, buildings
cultivated fields, orchard, improved road, major highway, unimproved dirt road

What Should Elementary-Age Children Learn About Geography?

Geography has long been considered one of the major pillars of the social sciences and therefore of the social studies. History presents information from the perspective of time; geography adds the dimension of location. Elementary-age students, particularly those in the early years, understand "location" better than "time." Thus, geography is a natural starting place in overall knowledge from the various social-science disciplines.

Children in grades K-6 should know locations of places and peoples (remember to keep a "people orientation "). They should understand why towns, cities, etc., are located in particular places, how people have shaped them, and how they have affected and continue to affect people's lives. Students should also be able to use knowledge of geography to solve problems and make important decisions in daily life.

Standards for Teaching Geography to Elementary-Age Students

The National Council for the Social Studies has published a framework of "standards" for *social studies instruction* in all grades. The standards present a model based on ten thematic strands for achieving excellence in elementary social studies teaching. This includes the area of geography. These standards provide direction for teachers addressing the "what" and "why" to teach children.

TEN THEMES WHICH SERVE AS ORGANIZING STRANDS FOR ELEMENTARY SOCIAL STUDIES CURRICULUM

I.   **Culture**
II.   **Continuity and Change**
III.   **People, Places, and Environment**
IV.   **Individual Development and Identity**
V.   **Individuals, Groups, and Institutions**
VI.   **Power, Authority, and Governance**
VII. **Production, Distribution, and Consumption**
VIII. **Science, Technology, and Society**
IX.   **Global Connections**
X.   **Civic Ideals and Practices**

Using our earlier definition of geography--describing the earth, and especially describing the earth and its people--mark each strand you think includes "geography" as an area of inquiry. As you probably noted, geography could be a strand interwoven into *each* of these themes, but it is especially relevant to content in numbers I, III, VIII, and IX.

In 1984, a Joint Committee on Geographic Education of the National Council for Geographic Education (NCGE) and the Association of American Geographers (AAG), also produced five themes. They were also endorsed by the National Geographic Society. They are outlined in greater detail in the NCGE/AAG publication *Guidelines for Geographic Education, Elementary and Secondary Schools* (see references at end of this section) .

These standards reflect the scholarly contributions of geography to student learning. The standards include what young people in the United States should know and be able to do in geography. The true test of using a content standard from geography is its application with students in classrooms.

FIVE THEMES OF GEOGRAPHY FOR ELEMENTARY SCHOOLS

1. **Location — *Where is it?***
2. **Place — *What is it like?***
3. **Human/Environment Interactions — *Shaping the landscape***
4. **Movement — *Staying in touch***
5. **Regions — *'Worlds within a world'***

As you can see, the specific themes of the NCGE/AAG closely align those for social studies listed by the National Council for the Social Studies. These themes, or standards, offer a useful organizing framework for identifying relevant content taught to children.

A recent survey revealed that one in five Americans between the ages of 18 and 24 could not locate the United States on an outline map of the world. Integrating geographic understanding into the elementary school curriculum by meaningful lessons will help prevent this gross lack of understanding. As emphasis is placed on geographic themes through application activities on a day-to-day basis, factual understanding and enlightenment will occur. Maps, globes, and atlases should be daily resources to answer questions about people, where they live, how weather affects them, where they move, what characteristics they have because of where they live, and a myriad of other important "life" questions.

A Suggested Framework for Geographical Understandings

An adaptation of the themes referred to earlier, *as appropriate for elementary-age pupils,* follows. These themes are presented for your own understanding and the building of your geographic framework. They will also assist you, as a teacher, in organizing instruction for your students. The emphasis of the themes in this publication is on the *content* of geography. Each theme includes a question or two to help you, as a teacher, focus your own and children's thinking geographically. As you study further, and take the next step of selecting appropriate teaching activities, you will hopefully be thinking geographically and thereby promote thinking geographically with your students, to inspire them to investigate location, to note physical and cultural interactions, and to understand and work for positive environmental interactions.

Location--understanding the *positions* of people and places on the earth's surface. Where in the world are places located?

The theme of "location" offers a starting point. It asks the question, "Where is it?" When using a map, latitude and longitude help pinpoint the exact location of a place on the globe. Knowing a global address, and being able to read and follow a map, should enable anyone to find a location on the earth. Every point on earth has a specific location as determined by an imaginary grid of lines designating latitude and longitude. Parallels of latitude lines measure distances north and south of the line we call the Equator. Meridians of longitude lines measure distances east and west of the line we call the Prime Meridian.

Finding an exact (or "absolute") location of a place is only part of the story. It is also important to know how that place is related to other places ("relative" location). It is important to recognize interactions which occur between and among places. Places are connected in many ways--by land, or water, or even by technology in today's world.

Globes, maps, photographs, and other "visuals" are primary tools for investigating relationships between people, places, and environment. Children in elementary schools can begin at very early ages to use maps and globes. Even five-year olds can construct three-dimensional maps of the classroom to begin to understand symbolic representation and spatial relationships.

Students in elementary grades should be able to locate the following examples of "location."

- the highest mountain in our state or on our continent
- he national park nearest our town
- the mouths of two or three major rivers
- three major cities in the USA
- the capital cities of three foreign countries.

Please note: It is important in elementary grades to differentiate between towns and cities, states and nations, countries and continents, lakes and oceans. Misunderstandings concerning these "locations" often continue on through adulthood if not clearly established in the early years.

In the upper grades, students may progress to identify human-migration routes, weather patterns, economic concerns related to specific locations, communication networks, or systems of transportation.

Place--understanding the physical and cultural characteristics which distinguish one place from other places.

Just as each person has a unique personality, so does each place. The "place" theme investigates the physical and cultural features which gives a place or area its identity. What makes *this* place special or unique? What land forms, bodies of water, and other physical features are characteristic of this place? What are the distinctive cultural features?

Geographers describe places by both physical and cultural characteristics. Physical characteristics include such elements as mountain ranges, rivers, and animal life. Cultural characteristics include land use and ownership, town and city planning, building architecture, transportation and communication networks, and patterns of livelihood.

Languages, religious and political beliefs and ideologies, also shape the character of a particular location. Studied together, the cultural and physical characteristics of places provide clues to help us understand the nature of places on the earth.

We, as people, are attached to a particular place and region. Regions and places have been given meanings by people, and in turn those places and regions help people to organize and understand our world. An educated person knows and understands the physical and cultural characteristics of places, that people create regions to help categorize the earth's complexity, and that culture and experience influence people's perceptions of places and regions. In the lower grades, students might learn the words and sing "Home on the Range," to begin a conceptual understanding of "place." What kind of a place is this? What are it's physical and cultural characteristics? What others songs might they sing which describe particular places?

Students in grades three and four, could make a list of common phrases that include the world "place" (e.g., "to put someone in their place," "a place for everything and everything in its place," "caught between a rock and a hard place"). Do these and other phrases imply cultural and physical characteristics? Why are we comfortable in some places but not in others?

Upper elementary age students might pick a state or a nation. What kind of place is it? What unique qualities best represent this place? Further investigations might include places of historic or current natural disasters, cultural crisis, etc.

Relationships Within Places (Human/Environment Interactions) -- understanding the relationships within places; interactions of people with their environments that shape the characteristics of peoples and places.

How people respond to and modify their environment is a central focus of the "human/environment interactions" theme. What are the *interactions* among people and places which explain how we shape and are shaped by our environment? How have we used resources in our environment? Does climate affect ways of living? How have people changed their environment?

Interactions of people with "places" on earth is constantly changing. Interactions of population and culture, with cooperation or conflicts, are some of the factors involved. It is important for adults and children alike to realize the interactions of these components for an overall basic understanding of geography.

"Environment" means different things to different people, depending on their cultural backgrounds and technological resources. For example, people might dam rivers to prevent flooding or to provide irrigation. This project should require consideration of the potential consequences--changes to the natural landscape, changes to fish and other wildlife habitats, etc. Studying the consequences of the human/environment interaction helps people plan and manage the environment responsibly.

What are some ways people affect their environment every day? (Driving cars, using water, disposing of garbage, smoking cigarettes). What are some ways people affect their environment through seasonal activities?

(Watering lawns, burning leaves, fishing, hunting). Comparing the two lists may lead people to change behaviors and improve their environment.

Comparing photographs and maps of a town or city "then and now," portrays ways people have changed over the years. More buildings? Different kinds of buildings? Differences in transportation? More or fewer trees? Other changes in the environment?

Stories of people who struggle to survive in an unexplored environment (*The Swiss Family Robinson, The Mosquito Coast)*, reveal how people learn to adapt to their environment. How and where do they find food? Clothing? Shelter? How does their environment change as they begin to create a home for themselves? Compare ways in which they adapt successfully or unsuccessfully. Identify areas in the world where people must adapt to a harsh environment if they are to survive.

Movement--understanding human interactions on earth--people, goods and services, products, and information--which affect the characteristics of places.

How people respond to and modify their environment is part of the theme of movement. What are the global *patterns* of movement of people, products, and information? How do people in your town and other places depend on each other? In this nation and others?

People interact with other people, places, and things almost every day of their lives. They travel from one place to another; they communicate with each other; and they use products, ideas, and information which come from beyond their immediate location.

People migrate, increase, decrease, or stabilize their numbers in different places, and develop patterns of living that distinguish one group from another. Other topics such as economic interdependence, and the forces of cooperation or conflict, are geographical understandings with strong ties to other social science areas.

Students in elementary grades should be able to recognize where resources are located, who needs them, and how they are transported throughout the world. The geography theme of movement helps us understand how we as a people are connected with, and dependent upon, other regions, cultures, and people in the world.

To illustrate the concept of movement, look under "Churches" in a phone book. What different religious groups are represented? What are the origins of selected groups? What influenced their movement to or within the

USA? What are cultural, political, and historical factors associated with these groups?

Examine the clothes and artifacts you have with you currently. How many were manufactured in other countries? How were they transported here? What are different ways that ideas travel from one place to another? (Music, literature, technology). What about censorship, geographic barriers, language barriers? What happens when people are not able to communicate?

Regions--how they *form* and *change*.

The "regions" theme helps organize knowledge about people and the land they occupy. Looking at the world from the perspective of regions helps explain the differences between places or relationships between them.

The study of region is a basic unit of geographic study. Regions are areas of the earth's surface defined by certain unifying characteristics. They may be physical or cultural. Using the theme of regions, geographers divide the world into manageable units of study.

How might we divide the earth into regions to help us understand *similarities* and *differences* of peoples and places? Cultural regions? Physical regions? What are the unifying features of the Corn Belt? The Pacific Rim?

Geography provides a means to look at the past, present, and future. Events and issues, regardless of their past, present, or future, have a geographical context. Geography sometimes helps us interpret the past. We also can apply geography to interpret the present and plan for the future. History has witnessed many examples of people interacting with their environment. Some people adjust their lives to fit environmental conditions, while in other settings they greatly alter the natural environment to meet their needs.

Gulliver's Travels is set in a fictional region where everything is enormous. How do the geographic characteristics of Brobdingnag make it different from other regions in the story? Are there other stories with unique geographical characteristics that identify a "region?" How do grasslands, deserts, rain forests, mountains, polar regions differ? How are they the same? What would we need to do to adapt to life in each one? (e.g., food, clothing, insects, ice). What are some unifying characteristics? What regions exist in our own town or city? How have regions in our city, state, nation, changed in the last 200 years? 100 years? 50 years? 10 years?

Organizing Conceptual Frameworks for Studying Geography

There is much to know about geography. However, "dumping the whole load" is neither necessary nor advisable in the elementary years. At this particular age, it is important to develop broad concepts and generalizations, which lay the groundwork for further understandings in later years. To illustrate, it is easy to be caught up in the pitfall of overemphasizing facts in geography, so much so that the broader conceptual learnings lay undiscovered. Geographic instructions for many of us formerly meant memorizing lists of names and locations of states, their capitals, imports and exports of various world places, without knowing the underlying reasoning associated with such information. Involving students of all ages in critical thinking, problem solving, and inquiry, will help them know not only where things are located, but *why* they are there, and *what* the consequences of these locations might be. Developing in-depth learning on one or two major concepts has a much higher return overall than memorizing lists of names, products, and other geographical facts. Once students have in-depth understandings of several major concepts, they then can make their own valid comparisons. In short, they being to *think geographically!* This is especially true for the upper elementary grades. Thematic units, or integrated curriculum studies, lend themselves very well to in-depth study of selected cultures.

References for Further Understanding

ERIC Clearinghouse for Social Studies/Social Science Education
Web site: http://www.indiana.edu/~ssdc/eric-chess.html
Address: 2805 East 10th Street, Suite 120
Bloomington IN 47408-2698
(800) 266-3815 or (812) 855-3838
For a list of ERIC collections in your area, contact ACCESS ERIC at 1-800-LET ERIC
Sample documents available from ERIC:
- Framboluti, Carol Sue (1991). *Helping Your Child Learn Geography.* Washington, DC: US Department of Education. ED 313 316
- *Geography for Life: National Geography Standards* (Washington, DC: Geography Education Standards Project).
- *Guidelines for Geographic Education.* Washington, DC: Association of

American Geographers and the National Council for Geographic Education. ED 252-453
- *K-6 Geography: Themes, Key Ideas, and Learning Opportunities* (Geographic Education National Implementation Project (1987). Macomb, IL: National Council for Geographic Education. ED 288 807
- Natoli, S. J., Boehm, R. G., Kracht, J. B., Lanegran, D. A., Monk, J. J., & Morrill, R. W. (1984). *Guidelines for Geographic Education: Elementary and Secondary Schools*. Washington, DC: Association of American Geographers and National Council for Geographic Education.

National Council for Geographic Education
A major national professional organization for educators interested in geography . (NCGE). Publishes a *Journal of Geography*. A subscription is included as part of the annual membership fee. Many issues feature articles describing imaginative approaches to teaching geographic content to elementary age students. For more information, contact: National Council for Geographic Education, NCGE Central Office, Indiana University of Pennsylvania, Indiana, PA 15705

Geographic Alliance Network
A part of the National Geographic Society. Contact your state education office to determine if you have a state alliance. Each alliance draws together geographers and teachers. An alliance coordinator helps to organize activities and disseminate information. Most alliances sponsor summer geographic education institutes, one or two-day workshops, and the development of high-quality instructional materials. Contact: Geographic Education Program, National Geographic Society, Washington, DC 20036.
Web site: http://www.nationalgeographic.com

CIVICS

Dr. Bruce E. Larson
Western Washington University

Civics is the study of the duties, responsibilities, and rights of citizenship. The purpose for learning about civics (and political science) is to encourage civic participation and civic competence. The National Council for the Social Studies curriculum standards state that civic competence means developing "the ability to make informed and reasoned decisions for the public good as citizens of a culturally diverse, democratic society in an interdependent world" (p. 3). Knowledge of the structure and function of government, and of the duties and responsibilities of democratic citizens is the content focus of civics, and learning this content is a step toward preparing children to hold the "office of citizen." This "office" is important for all to hold in a society organized under the democratic ideal that has citizens share in the governance of a country. The values, attitudes and skills needed to be participating, civic-minded citizens include:

- Democratic values such as equality, justice, human dignity, respect for the common good.
- Democratic attitudes such as participating in public life/policy making, to critiquing current practice.
- Democratic participation skills such as discussing public issues, decision making, volunteering.

The Center for Civic Education developed the National Standards for Civics and Government. These standards are helpful for providing *five questions* that organize the contents of this chapter:

- What is government and what should it do?
- What are the basic values and principles of American democracy?
- How does the government established by the constitution embody the purposes, values, and principles of American democracy?
- What are the roles of the citizen in American democracy?
- What is the relationship of the United States to other nations in world affairs?

While this is important content, the need to apply this knowledge and become participatory citizens is critical, and should begin in the K-6 classrooms.

What Is Government and What Should It Do?

"[T]hat this nation, under God, shall have a new birth of freedom; and that government of the people, by the people, for the people, shall not perish from the earth"

(Abraham Lincoln, Gettysburg Address, 1863).

Government is best thought of as **people and groups who have the right to make, apply, and enforce rules and laws**. Individuals and groups comprise the government, and will ideally have the interests of the country and the people being governed at heart.

The Center for Civic Education suggests that the governance of families and schools are analogous to local, state, and national governments. For example, parents make rules that govern the behavior and actions of their children. Parents are also responsible for enforcing the rules, modifying them, and addressing conflicts that arise because of them. School boards, administrators, and teachers make rules governing the actions and behaviors of a school. They also implement, modify, and settle disputes around these rules.

At the city level, city councils and mayors make, apply, and enforce rules for their communities; governors and state legislators do so for their states; and the federal government makes, applies, and enforces rules and laws for the nation. Tribal governments carry this out for tribal members on Native American tribal lands and sovereign nations. Courts at the city, state, and national level manage disputes, apply laws, and penalize lawbreakers.

The government has the authority to make, apply, and enforce rules and laws because citizens grant it that power. As the Declaration of Independence (1776) states, "Governments are instituted among Men, deriving their just Powers from the Consent of the Governed..." With that authority comes a degree of power. Citizens give the government authority and ascribe it power in return for the security, protection, order, and public services.

Governments also provide many public services to a society. In the United States, they help with services such as defense, funding schools and other service institutions, building libraries, hospitals, parks, and recreation sites, and keeping accounts of births, deaths, and myriad other records.

A lack of government structure will lead to anarchy, or lawless confusion. A classroom without a form of governance--without rules, or without a teacher/leader--would not be able to function adequately. A city, county, state, or nation would be equally impaired. Within a democracy, this structure is determined by the majority (they select the people who comprise the government), but any form of government (democracy, monarchy, dictatorship) serves to structure a society.

Rules and Laws

Rules and laws prescribe behaviors of people. Most rules and laws *protect people* (e.g., attend school and do homework, respect other peoples' privacy and property), *provide order* (e.g., raise one's hand and be recognized before speaking in class, obey traffic laws, enforce laws that protect people from others who want to harm them or take their property), and *protect rights* (e.g., the right to practice any religion, the right to equal opportunities for all students to receive an education).

In addition, rules and laws can also serve to assist citizens by *requiring benefits* (e.g., laws that provide for schools, health services, public transportation, highways), *requiring specific actions, duties, or responsibilities* (e.g., requiring people to pay taxes or perform military service), and in a democracy, *limiting the power of people in authority* (e.g., laws that prevent parents from abusing their children, term limitations on elected offices).

The quality, effectiveness, and fairness of a law ought to be constantly examined; this is one of the unique characteristics of a democratic government. As American citizens, we have the ability--and the requirement--to insure that laws attempt to meet core values of society, are possible to follow and enforce, and are not biased against or for any individual or group. The government could establish any number of laws and rules, but only those that the people deem appropriate are the ones that are enforced. The quickest assessment of rules and laws is to determine whether they are designed to protect individual rights and promote the common good.

Limited and Unlimited Government

The most exciting aspect of a democratic government is that everyone, including all of the people in positions of authority, must obey the laws. This is known as a *"limited government,"* because the authority and power of the government is limited by common laws and rules. Limitations are placed upon those in authority by the Constitution and Bill of Rights and numerous other laws. These limits are designed to protect fundamental values and principles and to insure that government serves the purposes for which it was established. Unlimited governments, by contrast, have no effective controls over those in power. Understanding of differences between limited and unlimited government provides a basis for making reasoned judgments about whether people in authority are acting in accord with the responsibilities they have been assigned and the limitations placed upon their powers. Limited government is critical in the protection of individual rights and freedoms. A democratic government requires a limited government, in which the laws and expectations of the society (the governed) are also imposed on the people elected or appointed to government office.

What are the Basic Values and Principles of American Democracy?
"We hold these Truths to be self-evident, that all Men are created equal,
that they are endowed by their Creator with certain unalienable Rights,
that among these are Life, Liberty, and the Pursuit of Happiness"
(Declaration of Independence, 1776).

The democracy in the United States of America has fundamental values, principles, and beliefs that provide common ground for Americans. *Values* are things people think are important or good. *Principles* are guidelines by which people govern their actions. *Beliefs* are those things in which we place our trust or confidence. While we are a diverse society, core values, principles, and beliefs serve to focus citizens on the attainment of common goals. Americans attempt to put these goals into action at the individual, local, and federal levels of government and day-to-day living. These values, principles, and beliefs are expressed in the "founding documents" such as the Declaration of Independence, the Preamble and United States Constitution, the Bill of Rights, the Gettysburg Address, the Pledge of Allegiance, speeches, songs, and stories.

Based on these documents, the Center for Civic Education developed the following list of fundamental *values* of American democracy.

Fundamental Values

- Individual rights to life, liberty, property, and the pursuit of happiness
- The public or common good
- Justice
- Equality of opportunity
- Diversity
- Truth
- Patriotism

In addition, they also describe the following fundamental *principles* of American democracy:

Fundamental Principles

- The people are the ultimate source of the authority of the government. "We the People..." have created the government, given it limited power to protect their rights and promote the common good, and can remove people from office and change the government.
- The power of government is limited by law.
- People exercise their authority directly by voting for or against certain rules, laws, or candidates as well as by voting in community or town meetings.
- People exercise their authority indirectly through representatives, who they elect to make, apply, and enforce laws and to manage disputes about them.
- Decisions are based on majority rule, but minority rights are protected.

Most of these cited beliefs and values come from the Bill of Rights. The first ten amendments to the United States Constitution comprise the Bill of Rights, written by the First Congress to limit the powers of the national government, and protect the rights of the individual citizen. Rights to freedom of religion, speech, the press, life, liberty, and property are granted in the Bill of Rights. Other beliefs and values, such as the individual rights, equality of opportunity, education, and voluntarism stem from this document as well.

Finally, the Center for Civic Education suggests that Americans need to hold in common the following *beliefs*:

Fundamental Beliefs

- All people have a right to equal opportunity in education, employment, housing, and to equal access to public facilities such as parks.
- All people have a right to participate in political life by expressing their opinions and trying to persuade others.
- All citizens over 18 years of age have the right to vote.
- Citizens who meet age and other qualifications have the right to seek public office.
- Everyone has the right to be treated equally in the eyes of the law.
- Everyone, including government officials, must obey the law.
- Education is essential for informed and effective citizenship, and for earning a living. Everyone should take advantage of the opportunity to be educated, and have a right to appropriate educational opportunities.
- Work is important to a person's independence and self-esteem, and to the well-being of the family, community, state, and nation.
- People should volunteer to help others in their family, schools, communities, state, nation, and the world. Volunteering is a source of individual satisfaction and fulfillment.

To summarize, Americans believe that a fundamental reason for government is the protection of individual freedoms and rights. The government should also promote the common good, and be guided by majority rule (but still insure the rights of the minority). Individuals have the right to differ about politics, religion, or any other matter, and can express their views without fear of being punished by their government or other citizens. They are also assured equality of opportunity, and equal protection under the law. To this end, everyone should be concerned about the well-being of his/her community, state, and nation.

Democracy and Diversity

Democracy, specifically the United States of America's government structure, is so unique that it has often been referred to as a great experiment in power, authority, and government. The idea that a government would be based on the direction and wishes of the people was drastically different than the monarchy (e.g., a king/queen ruled government) against which the early

Americans revolted. Add to this idea of a citizen-ruled government the fact that America is not comprised of a single race, ethnicity, or religion. The challenge of a democracy then becomes determining how an extremely diverse group of citizens can share the governance of a nation. Certain values, principles, and beliefs serve as a rallying point for a democratic society.

In contrast to most other nations, Americans do not share a single ethnicity, race, religion, class, or national origin. Instead, Americans share core values, principles, and beliefs. These shared values, principles, and beliefs help Americans find common ground as they interact. The very slogan E Pluribus Unum (translated as "from the many, one) is a call for Americans to be unified in purpose and principle, not to be the same type of person. What are the benefits of being in a nation of "many?" Diversity fosters a variety of viewpoints, and fresh ways of looking at and solving problems, it provides people with choices in the arts and literature. Diversity helps people appreciate cultural traditions and practices other than their own.

American holidays such as the Fourth of July, Labor Day, Memorial Day, Presidents' Day, Veterans Day, or Martin Luther King, Jr.'s Birthday help focus members of the U.S. society on commonly valued events and people. Explaining to students what these holidays represent, and why we celebrate them is important, if students (and citizens) are to begin feeling a sense that they share values, principles, and beliefs with others.

However, people in a diverse society may treat others unfairly based on their differences. Racial, ability, and/or religious discrimination are possibilities in any diverse society. Conflicts arising from diversity are inevitable. One of our central challenges is to find ways to practice the famous words of Martin Luther King, Jr. (1963): "I have a dream that my four little children will one day live in a nation where they will not be judged by the color of their skin but by the content of their character." We need to manage our differences, hold human dignity in high regard, and promote the common good and the protection of individual rights. To protect our own rights, we must be responsible for supporting the rights of others, even those with whom we may disagree or dislike.

How Does the Government Established by the Constitution Embody the Values, Principles, and Beliefs of American Democracy?

"We the people of the United States, in order to form a more perfect Union, establish justice, insure domestic tranquility, provide for the common defense, promote the general welfare, and secure the blessings of liberty to ourselves and our posterity, do ordain and establish this Constitution for the United States of America"
(Preamble to The Constitution of the United States, 1787).

The United States Constitution--What and Why

The writers of the Constitution outlined six goals in the Preamble: 1) set up a stronger central government than they had since Independence from Britain; 2) improve the judicial/court system; 3) promote peace among and within the states; 4) protect the country from enemies; 5) promote the safety and well-being of the people; 6) keep freedoms for future generations of Americans. Following the Preamble are the seven articles of The Constitution (which serve as a plan for government), and the amendments to The Constitution (which serve to revise or change the original document).

The United States Constitution (1787) is the plan for government in the United States. It is the written document that establishes the government as a *service* to the people, not as an unlimited, powerful authority. In the Constitution, an organized government is established to protect the rights of individuals, and to establish a peaceful, orderly society. All laws must be in accordance with the Constitution. The United States Constitution is the highest law in the land; no local, state or federal government can make laws that take away the rights it guarantees. No citizen--not even the President--is above the law, and all are expected to obey to the law. The writers of the Constitution believed that government is established by and for the people, government is the servant of the people, the people have the right to choose their representatives, and the people have the right to change their government and the United States Constitution. The Constitution sets forth these purposes, and provides a basis for understanding the fundamental ideas underlying government and evaluating its actions.

National Government

The national government established by the Constitution is responsible for making, carrying out, and enforcing laws that serve the purposes for which it was established--the protection of individual rights and promotion of the common good. It is also responsible for seeing that disputes about laws are settled in a fair manner. To accomplish this, the powers and duties of the government is divided into three branches: 1) legislative; 2) executive; 3) judicial. The purpose of this separation is to prevent a person, or group, from gaining all the power. Each branch holds the other two branches accountable, and serves as a "check and balance" on the others. The *legislative* branch passes laws, the *executive* branch enforces the laws, and the *judicial* branch settles conflicts arising from the laws. At the national level, the day-to-day activities of these three branches occur mainly in Washington, DC.

Legislative Branch. Congress is the legislative branch, and is made up of the Senate, and the House of Representatives. Congress passes laws to protect individual rights (e.g., laws protecting freedoms, and preventing unfair discrimination), and promote the common good (e.g., laws providing for clean air, national parks, and the defense of the nation). The Constitution establishes the rules Congress must follow, as well as the requirements to be a member.

The Senate has two members from every state who are elected for a term of six years. Each senator represents his/her entire state. The House of Representatives has 435 members. Every ten years based on censure information about the population, Congress decides how these 435 representatives are divided among the states. This is the way that the House of Representatives attempts to establish equal representation. Representatives in the House are elected for two-year terms. Unlike senators, they do not represent the entire state, but represent "congressional districts;" divisions within a state that attempt to divide the population evenly among all the representatives.

Executive Branch. The President of the United States is the executive branch of the government. The President's primary job is to carry out the laws passed by Congress. In addition to being the Chief Executive, The President heads the military (as the Commander in Chief), directs foreign policy, and provides direction on domestic policy (primarily the laws and policies that Congress considers each year). The President is elected for a four-year term, and can only serve two elected terms.

Judicial Branch. Federal courts are the judicial branch of government. The United States Supreme Court is the head of this branch, though lower courts can be created to help in the work of the judicial branch. Federal courts consider cases that challenge laws for there adherence to the Constitution. Judges are appointed, and often have the option of serving a "life-long" term in their position.

The Three Branches and Laws. Laws are made when legislators introduce a bill with the intention of making a new law. Only about 5% of all bills make it through the process of being approved. Most of the process occurs as the bill is examined, amended, and refined in Congress. If it passes through both the House and Senate, the President either signs it into law, or vetoes (rejects) all or parts of the bill. The judicial branch stands ready to mediate confusion or challenges to a law.

State Governments

State governments are established by state constitutions, which have purposes and functions similar to the United States Constitution. Copies of State Constitutions are readily available from your state governor's office, or from your local representative. Each state has its own legislative, executive, and judicial branch. State governments create and carry out laws for such issues as providing for public education, health care, parks, roads, and highways. As is the case at the federal level, the state legislative branch engages in activities such as making state laws, deciding how the state will spend tax money, and approving appointments made by the governor. At the state level, the executive branch is led by the governor. It enforces laws made by the state legislature (e.g., laws providing for education, health care for needy children, protection of natural resources). The state-level judicial branch interprets state laws, and manages conflicts about state laws.

Local Governments

Local governments provide most of the services citizens receive, and local courts handle most civil disputes and violations of the law. State and local governments provide services such as: licensing businesses, professions, automobiles, and drivers; providing essential services such as police and fire protection, education, and street maintenance; regulating zoning and the construction of buildings; providing public housing, transportation, and public health services; and maintaining streets, highways, airports, and harbors. Local government services are paid for through property, sales, and other taxes, and through money from state and national governments.

Local governments generally are more accessible to the people than their state and national governments. Members of city councils, boards of education, mayors, and other officials often are available to meet with individuals and groups and to speak to students and civic organizations. Meetings of local agencies are usually open to the public. People can participate in their local government by being informed and taking part in discussions of local issues, voting, volunteering their services, holding public office, and serving on governing committees.

Who Represents You in Government?

Can you name the persons representing you (and your students' families) at state and national levels in the legislative branches of government (e.g., representatives and senators in their state legislature and in Congress)? Can you name the persons representing you at the executive branches of government (e.g., mayor, governor, president)? Can you explain how to go about contacting your representatives? In a representative government where citizens give authority to people who promise to represent them in government, it is important that you and your students learn how to find answers to the above questions.

What are the Roles of the Citizen in American Democracy?

"The well-being of American democracy depends upon the informed and effective participation of citizens concerned with the preservation of individual rights and the promotion of the common good. Americans have always engaged in cooperative action for common purposes. Participation in government, contrasted with the wider realm of organized social participation, has ebbed in recent decades, however. Indifference to or alienation from politics may characterize a significant segment of the population."

(Center for Civic Education)

The role of the citizen in an American Democracy is, in a word: ***active***. One goal of social studies education is to promote understanding about government to assist people in becoming participatory citizens.

A United States citizen is a legally recognized member of the nation. Each citizen has equal ***rights***, which are protected by law. The Center for Civic Education provides examples of three kinds of citizens' rights:

1. Personal rights: associate with whomever one pleases, live where one chooses, practice the religion of one's choice, travel freely and return to

the United States, emigrate.

2. Political rights: vote, speak freely and criticize the government, join organizations that try to influence government policies, join a political party, seek and hold public office.

3. Economic rights: property ownership, choose one's work, change employment, join a labor union, establish a business.

The primary civic role of American citizens is to preserve the protection of personal, political, and economic rights of individuals. Citizens also have certain *privileges* (e.g., receiving services and protection from the government) and *responsibilities*. Commonly held responsibilities of American citizens include:

- Serving their community, state, and nation
- Obeying the law
- Working to change laws that promote unfairness
- Respecting the rights of others
- Being informed and attentive to the needs of their community
- Critiquing elected leaders
- Communicating with representatives in their school, local, state, and national governments
- Voting
- Paying taxes
- Serving on juries
- Serving in the armed forces

Americans who are not citizens (often called "aliens") have many of the same rights, privileges, and responsibilities of citizens. However, they may not vote in elections, serve on juries, or hold elected office. People who are born in the United States automatically become citizens, with few exceptions such as children of foreign diplomats. Adults who have come to the United States can apply to become citizens after residing in the country for five years, passing a test about the United States Constitution and the history and government of the United States, and taking an oath of allegiance to the United States. Minors become citizens when their parents are naturalized.

In an American Democracy, the people hold the "office of citizen," which carries with it personal and civic responsibilities. For American democracy to function, citizens not only must be aware of their rights, they must also exercise them responsibly and they must fulfill those responsibilities necessary to a self-governing, free, and just society. Since citizens share in the governance, they need to accept responsibility for the consequences of their actions, and recognize that their actions have implications on their country, and the continuance of a democratic government.

If citizens want their views to be considered, they must become active participants in the political process. Although elections, campaigns, and voting are at the center of democratic institutions, there are many other ways to be involved and active. Becoming informed about political issues, discussing public issues, contacting public officials, and joining interest groups and political parties are all effective ways to "be heard" and to become active participants in the political process. Because democracies depend upon citizen involvement, opportunities one could take advantage of include attending meetings of governing agencies (e.g., city council, school board), working in campaigns, circulating and signing petitions, and taking part in peaceful demonstrations.

In a government of a large nation, representatives carry the interests and desires of the people. Civic participation is important because representatives depend on being told, by the people, how they wish to be governed. A representative government, then, is restricted by the willingness of the people to communicate with their elected officials. Voting is an important part, but not the only part of being an active citizen. Also needed is a willingness and ability to interact with others, and with elected officials, about issues that are important to a democratic society.

What is the Relationship of the United States to Other Nations and to World Affairs?

What we call foreign affairs is no longer foreign affairs. It's a local affair. Whatever happens in Indonesia is important to Indiana....
Dwight D. Eisenhower (1959)

Since the world is divided into many nations, each with its own form of government, the possibility of conflict among nations/governments (and people) is strong. Each nation is made up of its territory, people, laws, and government. Each nation has its own set of norms, and cultural ideals. The democratic government under which we function in America is unlike the governments of many other nations in the world, yet the United States must interact with other nations (e.g., with economic issues such as trade and tourism, environmental issues such as pollution and conservation, and humanitarian issues such as child labor and oppression). The challenge is to resolve conflicts and maintain our own values, principles, and beliefs (e.g. to promote the rights of all people to life, liberty, property, and to promote the common good). These are clearly Democratic values and rights, however, so conflicts arise when interacting with nations that do not share these values.

Nations interact by sending representatives to meet together to discuss common interests and problems. This is often referred to as *diplomacy*. Representatives attempt to identify peaceful solutions, or to provide insight that will increase understanding among other nations. They often make treaties or agreements. For example, they might promise to defend one another, agree to protect the environment, or boycott another nation's import/export of goods and services. Nations also interact informally as people and the culture of one nation "visit" other nations. Tourism, international meetings, exchanges of students and teachers, and travelling art exhibits are examples of informal interactions.

Each nation has power and authority over itself. The *United Nations* (U.N.) is an international organization that provides a way for representatives of different nations to meet together to discuss their common interests and to attempt to solve problems peacefully. Sometimes the U.N. does this by sending peacekeeping forces to areas where there are conflicts, by organizing boycotts or embargoes, by drafting treaties or agreements, or by combining the militaries of the nations who are part of the U.N. and using force.

References For Further Understanding

The Center for Civic Education. The five standards used to outline the Civics chapter were from the *National Standards for Civics and Government* (Calabasas, CA: Center for Civic Education, 1994). This Center is a tremendous resource for curriculum materials, lesson ideas, and civic standards. The work of the Center is cited throughout this chapter on Civics. The mission of the Center is to promote informed, responsible participation in civic life by citizens committed to values and principles fundamental to American constitutional democracy.

They are located at: http://www.civiced.org
5146 Douglas Fir Rd.
Calabasas, CA, 91302-1467
phone: (818) 591-9321 / fax: (818) 591-9330 / e-mail:
center4civ@aol.com

National Council for the Social Studies. The NCSS themes "Power, Authority, and Governance" and "Civic Ideals and Practices" deal directly with Civics. These themes are located in *Expectations of Excellence: Curriculum Standards for Social Studies.* (Washington, D.C.: NCSS, 1994).

They are located at: http://www.ncss.org
3501 Newark Street, NW
Washington, DC 20016.
phone: (202) 966-7840

Close Up Foundation. The Close Up Foundation mission statement includes: "Close up is committed to developing new and better ways for young people, and teachers…to gain a practical understanding of how public policy affects their lives, and how individual and collective efforts affect public policy. Close Up conducts programs to increase civic involvement, promote civic achievement, and encourage civic awareness.

They are located at: http://www.closeup.org
44 Canal Center Plaza
Alexandria, VA 22314-1592
phone: 1-800-CLOSEUP (256-7387); TTY: 800-336-2167

CIVITAS: A framework for civic education. (1991) Charles N. Quigley, editorial director, Charles F. Bahmueller, general editor. Calabasas, CA : Center for Civic Education.

This book is a curriculum guide to revitalize civic education in schools throughout the nation. It describes national goals to be achieved in a K-12 civic education curriculum. Teachers will find lessons and curriculum ideas.

ECONOMICS

Dr. Jack Morgan
University of Louisville

Economics is a way of thinking. It is a commonsense procedure for solving problems, for making thoughtful choices among alternatives. It is not a collection of terms to be defined and memorized. The discipline does use economic concepts, but they are interrelated and applied in economic thinking. There is a strong need for understanding economics because it is such an important part of our everyday lives. In a 1999 Louis Harris survey of adults 18 years and older, it was found that they lack a basic understanding of money, scarcity, and inflation. Over 60% of adults incorrectly believe that money maintains its value during inflation.

The voluntary national content standards for economics are closely interrelated, as you will see. This chapter discusses 17 of the 20 national content standards in economics. Three standards are not included in this chapter because the benchmarks for these standards are for the twelfth grade only. The three omitted standards are about: how changing interest rates affect the allocation of resources, Standard 12; economic policies of government, Standard 17; and the role of the federal government in carrying out fiscal policy and the role of the Federal Reserve system in carrying out monetary policy, Standard 20. The National Council on Economic Education in a partnership with the National Association of Economic Educators, the Foundation for Teaching Economics and the American Economic Association Committee on Economic Education developed the content standards in economics.

Standard One: People in different societies are not able to satisfy all their wants for goods and services because resources to satisfy these wants are limited; therefore, they must make choices, satisfying some wants and not satisfying others.

Everyone seems to have unlimited wants for a limited amount of goods and services. This condition is called *scarcity*. We want tangible things such as shelter, food, clothing, cars, books, and games. It goes on and on. Economists call these tangible things *goods*. We also want intangibles such as entertainment, police protection, medical care, education, and leisure time. These intangible wants are called *services*.

Because of scarcity or the conflict between our unlimited wants for goods and services and the limited resources to satisfy these wants, people are continually involved in making choices. This occurs many times everyday. People who are involved in making these choices are called *consumers*. Would you rather have the summer vacation or a new computer? Would it be better to eat out or carry a lunch from home? Should I study tonight or watch my favorite television show? Would it be better to rent or buy a house? If I decide to watch my television show, tomorrow's homework will not be completed. In all of these problem situations, whenever one alternative is chosen, something else is given up. Economists call what is not chosen *opportunity cost*. Opportunity cost is whatever is given up—it is the next best choice. Think about it—if everyone could have everything they wanted, there would be no scarcity problem and opportunity cost would not exist.

People who make the goods and services consumers want are called *producers*. Producers try to produce the goods and services people want. They receive signals for what people want by the way consumers spend their money. If people have the drive and ability to buy more computers they will spend more money for computers; and therefore producers will try to make more computers. As consumers make choices, they are regularly interacting with producers. To produce goods and services, producers use three types of resources: (1) *Natural resources* include "gifts" from nature such as land and minerals. Natural resources are present without any human involvement. (2) *Human resources* refer to the jobs people perform to produce goods and services. Examples include dentists, barbers, teachers, and farmers. (3) *Capital resources* are goods producers make to produce other goods and services. They include tractors farmers use, trains and trucks that haul goods and services, and machines in factories that are used to make goods for consumers. Once producers know what goods and services consumers want, they are continually deciding the best or least-cost combination of the three kinds of productive resources to produce the desired goods and services.

Something To Think About:
Name the opportunity cost for a consumer choice you recently made?

Standard Two: The decision making process involves analyzing the benefits (positive characteristics) and costs (negative characteristics) for each alternative considered.

A good choice would be choosing the alternative that has the greatest benefits relative to the costs. Evaluation of alternatives is subjective. One person may prefer a dog for a pet; another may prefer a cat for a pet. One person may choose to live in the suburbs while another may prefer to live in the city.

When we make choices we make them in different economic roles. Consumers try to choose what they think will give them the most satisfaction. Producers try to produce what consumers will want to buy. Savers try to choose among alternatives after considering risk and comparing interest rates. Citizens apply this decision making process when they have the opportunity to vote for referendums, or for political candidates that take particular positions on economic issues. In almost all economic decisions, and in all these economic roles, there are pluses and minuses for each alternative. The best choice is the one that is believed, at the time the choice is made, to provide the greatest satisfaction to a want.

Something To Think About:

Analyze past purchases. Did you consider the costs and benefits before making the choices?

Standard Three: Goods and services are allocated in a variety of ways. Individuals, groups, and governmental units must all face the problem of scarcity and consequently, must make economic decisions.

Standards One and Two have described and illustrated how individuals are regularly involved in making economic decisions for themselves. These individual decisions are characteristic of a *market economy*, which largely characterizes our own economic system.

Other types of economic systems are *traditional* and *command* economies. In traditional economies, economic behavior is passed down from generation to generation by custom or ritual. The Inuits in Canada teach their children necessary skills for fishing and hunting. The giving of gifts for birthdays is an example of tradition in our modern economy. In the third type of economic system, the command economy, a central authority makes allocation decisions. For example, in the former Soviet Union the central government mainly determined which sectors of the economy would be the highest priorities. This is generally true in Cuba today. In reality, most economies have some characteristics of all three types.

There are many ways an economic system makes economic decisions about how to allocate goods and services. Examples in our economy include lotteries, first-come-first-served, contests, majority vote by a group, sharing equally, and by authority. To illustrate the latter, some teachers tend to be more authoritarian while others involve students more in deciding how time will be used on the playground.

Group economic decision making is illustrated when a community tries to decide about the use of a vacant lot. Would there be more benefits using the area as a playground for youth or should a new business be encouraged to locate there? How should an unused part of a schoolyard be used? Would it be better to develop an outdoor classroom or should the playground area be expanded? In making this kind of economic decision sometimes public meetings are held to allow the pluses and minuses of each alternative to be considered by the general public before the decision is made.

The same problems of scarcity and economic decision making are involved with economic decisions that governments make. Should the limited amount of tax revenues be used for roads, defense, or improvements in education? Because of limited resources, it would be impossible to provide enough revenue to fully fund all these.

Probably any system for allocating goods and services has some benefits and costs, but all economic systems must answer the basic questions: What *goods and services to produce? For whom will these goods and services be produced? How will these goods and services be produced?* Something To Think About:

Identify personal, group, and government economic decisions.

Standard Four: People respond to incentives in predictable ways. Both positive incentives (rewards) and negative incentives (punishments) affect people's behavior.

Students do chores at home for income, a prize, or to avoid punishment. People work to have an income to spend for goods and services and to avoid poverty. Businesses produce goods that consumers want in order to recover production costs and make a profit. If they fail, they lose money and eventually go out of business. Wages and salaries, prices for goods and services and productive resources, profits, and subsidies are all examples of economic incentives.

Employees leave one job for another to earn higher pay. Businesses shift production from goods consumers do not want to goods consumer want in hopes of making more profits. Wants are continually changing. People differ in the way they respond to incentives. To some, higher pay is most important. Others may work for less money because they experience greater job satisfaction in another position or they like the location where they live. In other words, incentives are not only monetary. For example, students may want to work hard to make good grades.

Something To Think About:

What positive and negative incentives cause you to respond in predictable ways?

Standard 5: Voluntary exchange between parties occurs when both parties believe they will benefit by the exchange. This applies to individuals, groups, and nations.

The simplest and oldest form of voluntary exchange is *barter*. In barter, there is a direct exchange of goods and services. If you want a certain good or service you must first find someone who has what you want. Then it is necessary to have what that person wants in a quantity and value that will be equal to what you want. The barter system is not very efficient although barters do occur in modern economies.

Figure 1 shows the flow of goods and services from producers to consumers in a barter economy. It also shows the flow of productive resources from the consumers as suppliers and owners of productive resources to the producers. Consumers own and rent property, own natural resources, own shares of stock in corporations that own capital resources, and consumers sell their human resources as members of the labor force.

Figure 1.
Circular Flow of Economic Activity

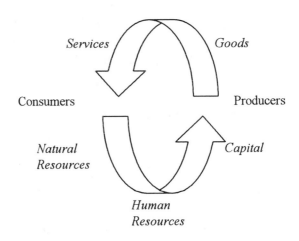

As societies become complex, money is most often used in voluntary exchanges. Whether exchange is a barter arrangement or involves money, both parties to the exchange think about the anticipated consequences if the exchange is completed, and they both believe that they will be better off giving up what they have for what they want. Later they may be disappointed, but at the time the exchange is completed, they believe the benefits of what they want outweigh the losses of what they plan to give up.

Individuals benefit from voluntary exchanges. Similarly, groups and even nations benefit from voluntary exchanges. Free trade increases the standard of living. For this reason, most economists favor free trade among nations without imposed barriers to imports and exports. Voluntary exchange is very important to the efficient functioning of an economic system.

Something To Think About:
How have you benefited from voluntary exchange today?

Standard 6: Producers are able to produce more when they specialize; therefore, consumers are able to consume more. Specialization leads to interdependence.

Specialization results in the more efficient use of the three kinds of productive resources—natural resources, human resources, and capital resources. This increased efficiency means greater *productivity*. Productivity is the amount of output in relation to the amount of input. Productivity increases when more goods are produced with the same productive resources. Greater productivity also occurs when the same amount of goods and services can be produced with less input of the three productive resources.

In today's modern economy, virtually all workers specialize. Some have natural abilities. Others have developed special skills. Teachers, farmers, carpenters, plumbers, salespeople, and doctors are specialists. They are usually considered more efficient, more productive, and superior in their specialized jobs. Because they spend most of their time working in a specialized job, such as teaching, they are dependent on other specialists to produce the goods and services they would be less efficient in producing. For example, dentists become dependent on teachers for providing a formal education for their children. This situation in which specialists are dependent on other specialists is called *interdependence*. Whenever there is specialization, there is necessarily interdependence. The greater the specialization, the greater the interdependence.

Henry Ford was one of the first businesspersons to benefit from specialization. In the early 1900's, he established an assembly line for building Ford cars. Each worker on the assembly line performed a specific task repeatedly. This *division of labor* resulted in increased productivity, i.e. more cars could be produced in less time. The cost of producing cars was reduced, and consequently the price of cars was less, permitting more consumers to buy new Ford cars.

Specialization and interdependence have many other applications. Regions, states, and nations specialize in producing goods and services. Specialization promotes trade among regions, states, and nations. Often, the natural resources in an area such as timber, oil, or coal, will cause an area to produce more of those particular products. Those products are then sold to other areas.

Something To Think About:

Can you name some goods or services that are specialized products in your community or state? Are they exported elsewhere?

Standard 7: Markets come into being when buyers and sellers interact, determine price, and allocate scarce goods and services.

Millions and millions of markets exist every day. A market relationship exists when both buyer and seller agree on the same *price*, what the buyer pays and the seller receives. When we go to the store and buy a gallon of milk, a market relationship is established. By paying the price stated, the market price, we agree, i.e. the buyer and the seller, that the price is just right. It is not too high (expensive) for the buyer or to low (cheap) for the sellers. Even if the buyer later complains about the price being too high, it really is unimportant because in purchasing the milk the buyer sends a true message that the price is right. In this situation, the buyer of the milk is the *consumer*. The seller of the milk is the *producer*. In fact, all those persons who are involved in processing, transporting, and selling the milk are producers.

Allocation in our market economy is determined by these many, many markets with prices determined by agreements about a common price among buyers and sellers. This is true for markets for consumer goods and services. It is also true for markets for productive resources (human resources, natural resources, and capital resources) that producers have to buy to produce the goods and services that consumers want. Examples of markets include face-to-face negotiations between buyer and seller at a car dealership; retail stores where the buyer sees the price of the good, picks it up and takes it to the checkout counter; and public auctions where the buyer is the person who is willing to pay the highest price. Other markets are more remote, such as catalogue orders that are mailed, telephone orders, purchases over the Internet, and the use of a credit card to buy gasoline at the gasoline pump island. In all of these examples, the market price is determined by agreements between individual buyers and sellers. The total effect of all these individual market relationships makes our economy function.

The relative scarcity of a good or service determines its price. If a popular toy, such as a Furby, is scarce or in short supply around Christmas time, consumers will bid the price up. In contrast, if there is overproduction of a particular model of a new car, the manufacturer will often offer a rebate or discount, in effect reducing the price. In this way, the market price is a clearing price. It is the price at which the quantity demanded is exactly equal to the quantity supplied.

Social Studies Content for the Elementary School Teacher p. 61

Something To Think About:

Think of some markets in which you have recently participated as a buyer or seller—as a consumer or producer.

Standard 8: Changes in supply and demand and in the number of buyers and sellers affect prices.

Prices seem to be dynamic, ever changing—at least for many goods and services. For most goods and services, as prices increase, consumers want to buy fewer units. There is an inverse relationship; as price increases the quantity demanded decreases. This principle also applies to producers' demands for human resources, natural resources, and capital resources, because producers are always trying to have the least-cost combination of these productive resources. As prices fall, consumers tend to demand more of those goods and services that have fallen in price and producers behave in a similar way. Producers will buy more raw materials that are used to produce goods when the price of those raw materials drop.

Producers behave differently when they supply goods and services consumers want. Generally, the higher the price for a good or service the more producers are willing to supply. To illustrate, a babysitter is usually willing to work more hours providing the service of babysitting if the pay is higher. Because of relatively high prices, producers of Beanie Babies were willing to produce even more Beanie Babies. In summary, the higher the price the smaller the quantity demanded by consumers, but the greater the quantity supplied by producers.

In this sense, price is a very powerful communicator in the marketplace. If the price for green beans would double many consumers would **substitute** another vegetable. If the price of gasoline increases significantly, many would try to reduce driving and in the long run, more small cars would be purchased. However, there is a big difference in the substitutability among products. Substituting one vegetable for another is relatively easy, but it is more difficult to find a substitute for gasoline. The basic principle is simple—we tend to be more sensitive to price changes for a product when there are close substitutes. When it is hard to find good substitutes and it is a product or service we believe we must have, we are less sensitive to price changes.

The demand for *complementary products* change differently when price changes. Goods are complementary when consumers tend to buy them together. Coffee and sugar are complementary, but coffee and tea are substitutes. Film and cameras are complementary to each other. If the price of cameras would increase significantly consumers would buy fewer cameras and the purchase of film would also decrease.

Something To Think About:

Can you think of a good or service that has recently changed in price? Did the price go up or down? How did you react? Did you buy it anyway or did you substitute something else?

Standard 9: Competition affects price. Competition among buyers causes prices to be higher. Competition among sellers causes prices to be lower.

Competition among buyers and sellers is an important characteristic of the United States economy. When people go to an auction, one of the first concerns is the number of people who are there. All these people are potential buyers. The more people the greater the likelihood prices will be high because buyers will bid prices up. Many buyers make the sellers and the auctioneer happy because buyers will be competing against each other. When a new toy or other popular product first comes on the market, many children and adults think they "just have to have it." They become somewhat insensitive to price and by purchasing large amounts of the new toy or product, they communicate a message to the sellers that the price is not too high.

Competition among sellers has the opposite effect. Competition lowers prices and generally the more sellers of the same or similar product, the lower the price will be. Sellers try to do what they can to make their products attractive to potential buyers. Having the lowest price can do this, but buyers consider other factors when making a purchase. Perhaps the seller is able to cause the product to be special or distinctive in some way such as greater convenience or an especially attractive package. Advertising is important when sellers compete. Consumers may be attracted to buy by the words, "new" and "improved." Advertising emphasizes special features in comparison with competitors' substitute products. To the extent buyers believe a seller's product is different, buyers become somewhat less price sensitive. Sellers may be willing to pay more if the product is believed to have special benefits, thereby providing greater consumer satisfaction.

Something To Think About:

What influenced you in a recent purchase? Was it price, advertising, brand loyalty, some special feature, or some combination of these factors?

Standard 10: Economic institutions are important in market economies because they provide valuable services to individuals and groups. Examples of economic institutions include banks, labor unions, nonprofit organizations, and corporations.

Banks are financial institutions that accept deposits and loan money. Bank customers have checking accounts, and they purchase certificates of deposits as a way of saving. *Savings* is the part of our income that we do not spend. Individuals often save for a specific purpose in the future, and banks pay interest on many of these accounts including certificates of deposit and negotiable orders of withdrawal (NOW accounts).

Banks also loan money to consumers and to businesses. Some loans are backed by the borrower's promise to repay. Other loans are secured with a form of collateral such as a home for a mortgage loan. Banks in the United States are important to the stability of our money and prices.

Labor unions are organized to promote the interests of workers. They represent workers in asking for higher pay and when disputes arise between workers and management. Members of unions pay dues to the union. The best-known and largest labor organization is the AFL-CIO or American Federation of Labor-Congress of Industrial Organizations. This economic institution is a federation of labor unions.

Nonprofit organizations make up a variety of economic institutions that do not include financial gain as the major goal. Examples include schools, churches, hospitals, and charitable organizations such as the Red Cross and Salvation Army. Since these organizations are not trying to make a profit, they are exempt from paying income taxes.

Business corporations are for-profit economic institutions. They are legally incorporated and recognized by the state of their incorporation. As legal entities they can own property, pay taxes, buy and sell property, enter into legal agreements, and sue and be sued. In short, they are legal persons and can do what individuals can do in the eyes of the law. The purpose of the corporation is to make a profit. Corporations are owned by shareholders whose ownership is represented by shares of common stock. Corporations distribute profits in the form of dividends to the owners or shareholders based on the number of shares each owns. Many but not all, of the familiar brand-name products that consumers buy at retail stores, are produced by for-profit corporations.

Something To Think About:

What contacts do you have with these economic institutions on a regular basis?

Standard 11: Money helps the economy operate more efficiently. Money provides a way of communicating common values when people buy, sell, borrow, and save.

Money is used when buyers and sellers exchange goods and services as well as productive resources. See Figure 2 and trace the circular flow of money between consumers and producers for goods and services *and* productive resources. Refer back to Figure 1 which represents the circular flow of goods and services and the three kinds of productive resources. Notice that money flows in the opposite direction in Figure 2.

Figure 2:
Circular Flow of Money

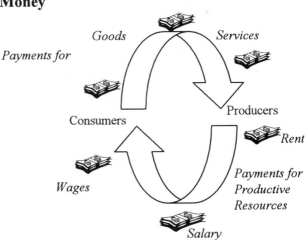

It is a convenient and efficient way to communicate value. "What did you pay for that?" "How much is that worth?" "How much did you get paid for that job?" Money replaces barter in modern economies because it is so much easier to communicate value. *Money* is anything that is generally accepted as payment for goods and services or for settlement of debt. Most of us want more money just like our wants for goods and services seem to be unlimited. Yet there is a big difference—money has value only because of the limited goods and services and productive resources it can purchase. Think about it. If more money is printed, money loses its value because the quantity of goods and services does not change. Prices go up—that is inflation.

Historically, money has taken many forms. During Colonial times tobacco, guns, corn, and wampum were used for money. Many colonies had their own currencies. The Revolutionary War was financed by Continental dollars—paper money. Today, our coins and paper money are backed by the full faith and credit of the federal government. There is no metallic backing, such as gold and silver, like there once was in the United States for our money.

Most nations have their own currencies. In Japan, it is the yen; in Canada, it is the dollar (with a different value from our dollar); in Mexico, it is the peso; In Russia, it is the ruble.

Something To Think About:

Imagine what it would be like if people had to barter for all the goods and services they purchased and for their work as members of the labor force?

Standard 13: Human resources, which is one of three productive resources, is provided by people in order for them to earn incomes.

The amount of income people earn depends on the market value of the goods or services they produce. When the market value is greater, those employers can afford to pay more, i.e. the demand for the productive work of those employees is greater. The income people earn also depends on the supply of workers. In recent years, there has been a large demand for employees with a variety of skills and backgrounds. Employees usually earn more income when they have special skills, education, or abilities, and these employees tend to be in shorter supply relative to the demand for them.

There are four different categories of workers – *unskilled*, *semiskilled, skilled*, and *professional*. Servers in fast food restaurants are unskilled workers. Semiskilled workers, such as dishwashers, have some mechanical ability and operate machines. Skilled workers are able to work with little supervision and run more complex equipment. An example would be a computer technician. Professional workers such as doctors and teachers have developed higher level skills and undergone more lengthy education and training. These four categories which comprise the United States labor force total almost 140 million people.

The work employees perform can be physical work or mental work. Whatever the kind of work provided, the employees must produce enough for the employer to at least cover the wages and salaries that are paid to them. Whether it is a server in a fast food restaurant or a famous movie actor, each must generate enough income for the employer to pay them for the work they provide. Employers must sell the produced goods and services at a price high enough to cover the costs for all three kinds productive resources—human resources, natural resources, and capital resources. Employers could not stay in business very long if they did not follow this principle.

Something To Think About:

Think about jobs that are known to you. What education, skills, and abilities are required? How do these characteristics relate to the incomes people receive who work in these positions?

Standard 14: Entrepreneurs are important in our economy because they employ the three kinds of productive resources to produce goods and services consumers want.

Entrepreneurs take risks, and if successful, earn profits. Edward T. Lewis is an entrepreneur. As head of one of the biggest African-American businesses in the United States, he is involved in publishing *Essence* magazine, book publishing, direct-mail marketing, and television production. Mary Kay Ash is an entrepreneur. She was the founder of Mary Kay, the well-known brand of cosmetics. Bill Gates is an entrepreneur. He founded Microsoft, and is one of the wealthiest people in the world. These people were innovators. They sensed what people wanted, invented it, and developed successful procedures and marketing strategies to satisfy those consumers wants.

Entrepreneurs also must work hard on difficult tasks, be creative, keep trying, and be willing to take calculated risks. Some fail because the invention does not work, because of difficulties in producing it, or because they misjudge how consumers will react to the invention. Successful entrepreneurs make profits when they are able to sell the new good or service for more than they pay for the productive resources to produce it. The profit motive is very important to entrepreneurs, but they also like being their own boss and being recognized for what they accomplish. Entrepreneurs contribute to economic growth because they employ productive resources thereby generating income for employees and the owners of other productive resources.

Something To Think About:

Identify some entrepreneurs in your community or state.

Standard 15: Savings and investing are important for people to enjoy a higher standard of living.

People save for many different reasons. They save for a "rainy day," for a vacation, for a down payment on a new home, for education, or for retirement. The money saved is usually saved in a way that earns interest. People are often faced with economic decisions about saving money. Should I spend what money I have *now* for something I want or should I defer my gratification and save to buy something *later* that costs more? The opportunity cost of having something now is not being able to have something in the future; the opportunity cost of saving for the future is not having something now. By applying the economic decision making process, the advantages and disadvantages of each alternative can be evaluated. Saving for the future requires postponing immediate satisfaction, sacrifice, and patience.

When people save in a bank and earn interest, banks loan this money to others who want to borrow money. Banks charge those who borrow money interest. Consumers borrow money to buy cars, to buy homes, and for education. Businesses also borrow money that is used for many different investments. They borrow money to build new manufacturing plants and to buy equipment such as computers, trucks, and machines. Often investment in these examples of capital resources makes workers more productive. When businesses are able to take advantage of new technology, it can cause productivity to increase. When workers are able to invest time and money in education and training, it can cause productivity to increase. Increases in productivity can mean a higher standard of living and general economic growth.

<u>Something To Think About:</u>
Trace how savings in the form of a certificate of deposit at a bank can contribute to a higher standard of living.

Standard 16: Government plays a valuable role in the economy when benefits are greater than costs. Government provides public goods and services and serves as regulators of many different economic activities. Government also collects tax revenues and spends or transfers monies received.

Examples of public goods and services provided by government includes roads, police protection, national defense, many elementary and secondary schools and universities, some health-care services, veterans benefits, and conservation practices, etc. The federal government provides some, such as national defense. Others, such as public elementary and secondary education, are primarily the responsibility of local governments. Still others, such as roads, are a shared responsibility among federal, state, and local governments. Generally, government provides those goods and services that the private sector in a market economy will not provide for itself, and public goods and services almost always benefit more than one person at a time.

Government is also a regulator. It enforces contracts. It promotes competition by prohibiting collusion that restricts competition among sellers. Restricted competition can cause prices to be artificially too high. Government watches for misleading advertising, regulates foods and drugs so they will be safe for consumers, promotes a safe environment by regulating pollution, and maintains national parks and forests.

For government to play these roles, it costs money. The annual federal budget is presently more than 1.6 trillion dollars. The largest expenditure for the federal government has historically been national defense; however, currently social security payments are larger than national defense. The largest expenditure for state and local governments is elementary and secondary education. Most of the revenue to pay for government comes from taxes. The sales tax is the largest source of revenue for state governments. The property tax and transfers from state and federal governments are the largest sources of revenue for local governmental units. The individual income tax is the largest source of revenue for the federal government.

Social Studies Content for the Elementary School Teacher p. 69

Something To Think About:

How many different kinds of taxes can you recall? How much government involvement in the economy should there be?

Standard 18: The total expenditures by a nation includes expenditures by individual consumers, businesses, or producers and governments. This total value is called Gross Domestic Product.

Gross Domestic Product (**GDP**) is the total dollar amount for all final goods and services produced by a nation in one year. GDP is reported quarterly by the Bureau of Economic Analysis, U.S. Commerce Department. It does not include the cost of intermediate products such as wheat that is used in cereal because the final price of the box of cereal *is* counted. In this way, double counting is avoided. It does not include people who clean their own apartments or houses because no one is paid for the service; however, it does include what a cleaning firm or individual is paid for providing the service of cleaning an apartment or home for someone else.

In 1998, GDP in the United States totaled $8.5 trillion. Considering its size, obviously GDP is not a perfect number, but it is the best overall approximate measure of the output in the United States. It is a valuable economic statistic and indicator of a nation's economic health. To illustrate its importance in another way, the definition of a recession is when GDP declines (after correcting for inflation or deflation) two consecutive quarters (three month periods). GDP is also valuable in comparing the economic growth rates of different nations.

Something To Think About:

Listen for media reports about the most recent quarter's GDP. What does it indicate about the health and future growth of our economy?

Standard 19: Inflation and unemployment are two serious economic problems. Inflation hurts many people, but sometimes benefits others. Unemployment hurts individuals and nations.

Inflation is an increase in most prices. *Deflation* is a decrease in most prices. The best known indicator of inflation is the consumer price index. The *consumer price index* measures general price changes at an annual rate and reports them monthly. The consumer price index is prepared by the Bureau of Labor Statistics. When prices go up, people who are hurt are those who work for wages and salaries, those who have savings accounts, those who have loaned money to others, and those who must live on incomes that are fixed, such as retirees. Those who may benefit from inflation include those who have borrowed money, those who work on commission, and those who can raise the prices for goods and services they sell without losing sales. The reason some groups are hurt and others gain during inflation is because of a change in the distribution of income and the general loss of purchasing power of dollars. Deflation is rare. There was significant deflation after World War I in the early 1920's and during the Great Depression during the 1930's.

Unemployed persons are people available and wanting to work. *Unemployment*, which is reported monthly by the Bureau of Statistics, is the percentage of the total labor force that is unemployed. Not only does unemployment work a hardship on those who are unemployed, it also means the economy is not as productive as it otherwise might be. And those people who are unemployed do not have the incomes to spend that they once had. This causes GDP to be less than it otherwise could be.

Political parties and leaders sometimes recommend different policy alternatives to deal with the economic problems of inflation and unemployment. Because of the widespread effect of inflation and unemployment, most people are affected by these government policies that attempt to alleviate the problems.

Something To Think About:

How does inflation hurt individuals and the economy in general?

References For Further Understanding

Giesbrecht, Martin Gerhard and Gary E. Clayton. (1997). *A Guide to Everyday Economic Thinking.* Irwin McGraw-Hill: New York.

This book describes the economic way of thinking. It explains how economists use description, analysis, explanation, calculation, and prediction to understand how people make economic choices.

Hazlitt, Henry. (1996). *Economics in One Lesson: 50th Anniversary Edition.* Fox & Wilkes: San Francisco.

This book looks at economics not just from the immediate effects of acts and policies, but also the long-term effects. It also traces the consequences of that policy not merely for one group, but for all groups.

Saunders, Phillip and June Gilliard, Eds. (1996). *A Framework for Teaching Basic Economic Concepts with Scope and Sequence Guidelines K-12.* EconomicsAmerica National Council on Economic Education: New York.

This book provides an explanation of basic economic concepts and methods. Basic economic vocabulary and analytical tools are included. Includes a scope and sequence guide for integrating the concepts within the k-12 curriculum.

Voluntary National Content Standards in Economics. (1997). EconomicsAmerica National Council on Economic Education: New York.

A guide for what K-12 students should learn about economics and the economy. Includes content standards, essential reasoning and decision making skills, rationales, benchmarks, and correlations.

The Federal Reserve homepage
    http://www.federalreserve.gov/ -- includes information about the Federal Reserve System, press releases, consumer and community information, reports to Congress, publications, and links to related websites.

The National Council on Economic Education's (NCEE) website
    http://www.nationalcouncil.org/ -- includes list of publications, announcements, interactive lessons, curriculum standards, and links to state councils and college/university economic education centers throughout the United States.